Becoming ENOUGH

FLOWER OF LIFE
PRESS

Voices of Transformation

Becoming Enough

Copyright © 2017 Amanda Johnson

This book is a seed. A seed that, when watered and nurtured and returned to again and again, might grow into a beautiful, soulful plant. There are no "get-[fill-in-the-blank]-quick" solutions. There are no guarantees that this seed will take root especially if the proper nutrients, care, and diligence are not given. It is through dedication and ongoing practice that these principles work. With that said, let's see what this seed can blossom into in your life.

The content of this book is for general instruction only. Each person's physical, emotional, and spiritual condition is unique. The instruction in this book is not intended to replace or interrupt the reader's relationship with a physician or other mental health professional. Please consult your doctor for matters pertaining to your specific health.

Cover and Intrerior design by Flower of Life Press

To contact the publisher, visit
FLOWEROFLIFEPRESS.COM

To contact the author or for permission requests, visit
WWW.AMANDAJOHNSON.TV

Library of Congress Control Number: 2017939404
Flower of Life Press, Lyme, CT.

ISBN-13: 978-0-692-87503-2
ISBN-10: 0692875034

Printed in the United States of America

Becoming ENOUGH

A
HEROINE'S JOURNEY
TO THE
ALREADY PERFECT SELF

AMANDA JOHNSON

PRAISE FOR *BECOMING ENOUGH*

"*Becoming Enough* is a book about daring vulnerability and joy, leaving the reader feeling empowered to explore."

–Sarah Caine, minister

"*Becoming Enough* is a truth-filled book about finally dropping your armor and all the trivial thoughts that keep you stuck and feeling small, leaving you feeling free—totally free. This book is a must-read for anyone who wants to unshackle themselves from the constant need for praise and obsession with getting better. I am already enough, and so are you."

–Jacqueline Fisch, jargon-free writer, editor, and author

"Eckhart Tolle says that the contribution of some of the greatest poets and artists of our time isn't to offer us a solution but rather offer us a reflection of the 'human experience and predicament so that we can see it more clearly.' This is exactly what *Becoming Enough* does by shining a light on the divine perfection that is carried within us all."

–Chelsey Dawn, transformational coach

"A must-read for every person struggling with their need for control and who wants to learn about surrendering to the perfect unfolding of life."

–Marjorie Warkentin, life coach and leader of women's circles

"Through the courageous sharing of vulnerable personal experience, *Becoming Enough* takes the reader on a hero's journey from a world built on comparison and self doubt, through the sometimes painful process of waking up to one's own inner truth, to ultimately a state of peace, acceptance, and inner prosperity. A must-read for anyone feeling stuck in their experience of 'not enough' looking to create more freedom and power in all aspects of their life."

—Mike Gittelman, personal transformation and business coach

"Whatever someone's journey is, wherever they are, they can certainly discover a part of themselves they may have forgotten or have recently relearned. Reading how Amanda trusted in her true self, how she evolved, encourages me as I learn to trust my own true self."

—Mike Huber, life coach and yoga instructor

"*Becoming Enough* offers relief from the grip of perfectionism and is a genuine celebration of everyone's divine goodness."

—Kathryn Tormos, Ph.D., question asker, soul searcher, and artist

"*Becoming Enough* shines the light on our 'perfectly human' nature and the role of judgment in our lives. It calls us to courageously venture into the dark night of the soul, lay down our armor, and journey to the inner sanctum where we awaken to the gifts of wholeness, inner knowing, and interconnectedness."

—Laurie Nelson-Moe, BCC, founder of Whole Life Balance Coaching and mindset mentor

"*Becoming Enough* is the incredible account of one woman's odyssey to find her happiness—her true North. One aspect of the archetype of The Heroine is described as 'using her new wisdom to restore fertility and order to the land.' Ms. Johnson has indeed accomplished this as she pays it forward in her book, inspiring and guiding others as they embark on their own quest to restore healing, growth, and order to their soul. This book is definitely a must-read."

–Lynn Darmon, spiritual medium

"*Becoming Enough* is raw, honest, and damn hard to put down. You may, like me, assume some of this book will pertain to you, only to open it and realize you are looking in a mirror, and it pertains to all of us. *Becoming Enough* is an unexpected guidebook. Never wagging its finger in our faces or telling us what to do, but inadvertently showing us, as we walk with the author through her own journey."

–Cara Viana Hollenbeck, spiritual teacher, healer, and coach

"*Becoming Enough* delivers a beautifully profound message to those constantly seeking to improve their lives through self-help, by guiding them to the realization that self-acceptance is the only thing we really need."

–Sarah Gallagher, founder of A Road to Bliss

"Full of wit and truth, *Becoming Enough* takes the reader on a well-crafted journey to the soul, offering freedom and security of knowing you are perfect just as you are!"

–Dr. Nathan Unruh, author of Strike It *and* DIGIT

"As a hummingbird artist who puts herself out there and transforms rejection into redirection on the daily, Becoming Enough is a must-read for fellow creative crusaders who want to feel whole within themselves first and heal those harsh voices inside their heads. It's a refreshing spin on self-help, ego medicine, and simply freeing for the soul. I can't think of one human not on this journey. Thank you, Amanda, for giving it a voice!"

—Tara Tagliaferro, stage actor, certified life coach, and gypsy soul

"She is courage, she is raw, and she is absolutely in full. Amanda Johnson takes the reader on a journey that is heartfelt and relevant. A masterpiece in truly becoming enough. In hearing her journey, we are left wanting. Wanting to know more. Driven to see what else we can learn in our own process of inquiry and elevation. Desiring to explore our own enough-ness. Johnson encourages us to take these steps knowing that we are not alone. Inspiring to say the least, and a must-read for anyone that is in search of their own inner strength and beauty. Bravo!"

—Hanz Kurdi, founder of Elevate Institute

"In *Becoming Enough*, Amanda Johnson meets you where you are—in perfectionism, doubt, and judgment of yourself—and guides you on a journey to trust, love, and acceptance. In a series of beautifully crafted stories and insights, Johnson encourages you to stop chasing perfection—and instead learn to see its roots already deep within yourself. A much-needed antidote in the often poisonous world of self-improvement."

—Sarah Rhea Werner, author and creator of the Write Now Podcast

For my parents, Scott and Marianne, who gratefully miscalculated on a summer day back in 1981. Thanks to you, I have proof that there is no such thing as a mistake.

You have not only been created, but have also been created perfect. There is no emptiness in you.

—A Course in Miracles

CONTENTS

A STATE OF POWERFUL
BEING PRECEDES A POWERFUL
STATE OF DOING.

—MARIANNE WILLIAMSON

ACKNOWLEDGMENTS

Nothing comes into being on its own. This book is no different. There are hundreds of people who played a role in the manifestation of this book. Many who I have the pleasure of knowing personally, others who I have yet to meet, and some who I will never have the chance but whose words inspired me across time and space.

Being my first book, I find myself struggling with who to thank by name given that there have been so many influential people in my life leading me to this point. Hundreds upon hundreds of teachers, mentors, guides, mirrors, supporters, cheerleaders, challengers, you name it. Since I can't list all by name, I am focusing on those who most actively were involved or directly influential in the creation of this particular book, though I recognize that each person I have had the pleasure of meeting along the way is part of my journey and why this book exists.

I will start with my innermost circle and work my way out. A huge thank you to my parents, Scott and Marianne Johnson, who, in a very literal way, made it possible for this book to be written. If it weren't for them, I wouldn't be here. In addition to giving me physical life, they have supported me emotionally, physically, monetarily, and spiritually along the way. Words do not do justice for how grateful I am. In addition, my mother played a significant role as my initial proofreader and there is no one else I entrust more with my words than her. I also want to thank my brother, Josh, for believing in me from the get-go and showing that in the form of investing in my personal development and opening up his home to me on multiple occasions, which served as a haven from which to write and create.

Words also fail to express my love and gratitude for my partner, Michael Delgado, and his unconditional love and support. From day one, he encouraged me to be me, accepted me fully, and allowed me to be exactly who I am. He is my teacher and mirror in countless ways. Our souls have known each other long before we met.

Then there is my dear soul sister, Tosha Smith, who played a vital role that I didn't even know I needed (and will now never do without for each subsequent book). She listened to me read each and every word of this book to her, offering her loving attention and brilliant feedback, bringing this book to a whole new level. I am so grateful for her time, energy, and creativity that took this book from something I am proud of to something I am really proud of.

I also want to thank my other soul sisters, without whom I would not be the woman I am today. I'll start with Jeannine Yoder who introduced me to many amazing women in my life whom she is one. I deeply appreciate how she shines her light so brightly giving others permission and guidance to shine theirs. In addition, I am beholden to my closest soul sisters—Elle Callanan, Marjorie Warkentin, Amy Biondini, Chelsey Verhulst, Stacey Cannon-Dykes, Hanna Bier, Marste McDonald, and Crystal Marsh—whose love, support, encouragement, and reflections serve as medicine and reminders of who I truly am on a regular basis. I love you all dearly.

I am in such deep gratitude to so many others who I consider part of my soul family, serving as constant inspiration and space holders for me. Our connections go deep (even if they are few and far between) and our conversations prompted much of what is in this book. A huge thank you to Wendy Lu, Kathryn Tormos, Hanz Kurdi, Gigi Azmy, Songya Kesler, Sarah Moore, Cara Viana Hollenbeck, Tara Tagliaferro, Shannon Ledford, Kelley Cooper, Angie Hauk, Luna Love, Emily Cassel, Fabiola Baylon, and many others whose names go unwritten here but are forever written in my heart.

My time in Peru—spent amidst the beauty of the land and people I shared my time with—was incredibly transformational. Much of what I experienced there served as lessons and offered me truths that made their way into this book. I sincerely want to thank my soul family who journeyed with me and offered me such a priceless gift of a lifetime. Deep gratitude to Cora Poage, Ginny Muir, Lindsay Annana Mae Wilson, Raj Aggarwal, Erin Derosa, Tammy Algera, Javier Regueiro, and Nora Dunn. You all have a special place in my heart forever.

Then there is my incredibly soulful publisher, Jane Ashley, who literally and figuratively helped deliver this book into the world. When Jane and I met, we just knew there was a reason and something special would be born of it. Our meeting was yet one more piece of evidence how I am not in control and am completely supported each and every step of the way. We met at exactly the right place at the right time, none of which was planned or could have been predetermined. Also, a huge thank you to my editor, Amy Paradysz, who, along with Jane, added a magic touch to this creative expression of truth.

I also want to thank Michelle James, my Creative Emergence coach, who guided me along the journey as I left the comfort and security of my corporate job and traveled into the wild Land of Non-Judgment. Thanks to her, I was willing to be uncomfortable and face fear at a critical time in my life. In addition, I want to give a special shout out to Stacy Kemp who served as a professional mentor and dear friend during a very pivotal time, when I chose between the path of comfort and the path of the unknown.

My gratitude is boundless for the many other incredible women and men who I have met along the way and who have held my hand (physically and figuratively), witnessed me, inspired me, cried with me, and shined their light on me a thousand times over. I trust you each know who you are and feel how deep of an imprint you have left on my heart and in my work.

I want to thank each of the 149 people who supported me in a monetary (and emotional) way by contributing to my crowdfunding campaign. Without each dollar given by so many generous souls, this book would not be in existence at this point in time. While the money was a necessary component, it was what the money represented that meant the world to me—each and every person's belief in me and in this book. My eyes filled with tears the day I reached my goal, mere hours before the campaign ended, and I still feel the joy and gratitude to this day. Thank you from the bottom of my heart to those who pledged their support, making this dream a reality. And a huge thank you to each and every person who has believed in me and this book and made it known in other forms. Your belief is a potent and powerful force. Never underestimate its power.

I also want to thank each and every person who has ever read my work, worked with me in one way or another, or shown interest in the message I am here to spread by breathing it in and sharing it with others. You are a such an important part of the ripple.

Finally, I wish to thank the incredible writers and spiritual teachers who came before me and whose words touched me so deeply, giving me the courage and energy to continue on my path.

Bringing something like this into the world is such evidence of how interconnected and interdependent we all are. While I celebrate my part in this, I could not have done it without the hundreds (if not thousands) of lives that directly and indirectly influenced me.

May this book serve as a reminder of the incredible impact we each have on others. Each action (or belief, or thought, or kind gesture, or loving word) creates a ripple that goes far beyond what we can ever imagine. Whether we've had just one conversation or we talk each and every day, thank you. What you do matters. And whatever you desire to do is possible. Just remember: We are all in this together and what you do is enough.

QUESTIONING ILLUSIONS
IS THE FIRST STEP IN
UNDOING THEM.

—*A COURSE IN MIRACLES*

PREFACE

I wrote this book because I have spent many years suffering and continue to witness the suffering of so many people around me.

I came to the conclusion that the suffering wasn't due to the fact that I hadn't yet accomplished something amazing, or didn't yet have a million dollars in the bank, or hadn't yet traveled to all the incredible places I wanted to travel. It was because I was totally unwilling to accept the truth of who I am, to witness my *enough-ness* as it is, to see that I am already complete in this very moment and there is no "there" to arrive at before I will stop suffering. I believe this very well might be the case for other people, too.

I tend to see patterns more than remember details. This book is a collection of patterns—me making connections over the course of my life with a few stories sprinkled in. But to me, it's not the story that is important. I know as a reader it can be fun to sink your teeth into someone else's experience through details and drama, but what I want to offer you is my experience of seeing these themes and patterns emerge in my life and how I have pieced them together. I don't want to get stuck in the stories—they are simply an opportunity to see the pattern, connect the dots, and see what needs to be healed. That's all.

This is what my journey—and this book—is all about. Exploring how these stories that turned into patterns have had an impact on my life, as well as learning to become friends with them so they no longer have such power over me. Along the way, I had to make friends with uncertainty. Part of this includes being willing to "not know," which is an interesting place from which to write a book. It asks that I share what I've experienced from a place of truth and vulnerability all the while knowing that I may not—actually, most certainly do not—have all the answers and never will, and, better yet, don't need to.

So then who am I to write a book about all this stuff?

Great question.

The way I see it is that part of my soul's work is to be a (somewhat obsessive) student of life, take lots of detailed notes, and share my experiences with others. That's not to say that my experience is "right" or the one-and-only answer. But sharing my experience may encourage you to ask questions of your own and reveal more of who *you* truly are. It very well may raise more questions than offer answers, which is okay, too.

My inability to appreciate my okay-ness in each moment led me on a search to constantly do more, have more, attain more, and sometimes be less, shine less, experience less. As far as I was concerned, I was never okay. I was never enough.

For so many of us, "enough" is not enough. It's reaching for low-hanging fruit and we can, nay, *should* reach for much higher fruit. Many of us immediately hear the word "enough" and think, "That's it? How will I ever accomplish anything worthwhile settling for 'enough'?" I had the same thoughts and reactions. Then I got honest with myself and realized that scoffing at "enough" was yet one more way of staying stuck in the illusion. "Enough" is the place to start. If you can't accept your enough-ness, you can never accept your magnificence.

I've spent nearly my entire life thinking there was a "right" and a "wrong," and I was most definitely doing it "wrong." This belief led me to years and years of disappointment, anxiety, depression, and pains-taking doubt. Over the course of my life, striving for external perfection was preceded by this belief that I'm not okay, I'm doing it wrong, I should be doing it better. Basically, I'm not enough, and all versions of that directed outwardly to other people or things.

Many of us are familiar with the idea that we are looking to somehow "fill the void" that we experience within. No matter what you label it, it all comes down to not feeling whole and complete just the way you are. So you think the answer lies in seeking it from others, because you don't notice you already *are* that which you seek. Then, you don't receive it because you aren't *being* it, and that perpetuates the belief that you don't have it within. What a vicious cycle! And one I know all too well.

My belief that I wasn't lovable or worthy has shown up in spending much of my life looking to others for their approval, affirmation, and opinion. I moved from one relationship to another (without taking time to develop a relationship first with myself). I spent many years as an actor looking for the praise and applause of the audience, working at a job and "doing what it takes" to move up the corporate ladder, and, more recently, looking to my Facebook page likes and number of views on my latest video to validate my worth.

I spent a lifetime feeling inadequate and incapable of listening to my own inner wisdom. I believed everyone else had it figured out, and I was failing big time. I assumed there was one way to do something, and it was their way, not mine. I thought, *If I'm to be "success-ful" or happy, I'd better be more like everyone else and do it their way.*

Here's the thing. I now experience what it's like to live without the constant need to improve myself, or search outside myself, or feel inadequate because my way looks different from someone else's. I'm learning to see myself as perfect just the way I am. And not "perfect" as in "free from faults or defects" but as in the less common, and yet primary, definition, "having all the required or desirable characteristics; as good as it is possible to be." I'm learning to trust myself and move forward despite uncertainty. I'm learning to see how connected we all are and how my way is just as relevant as anyone else's.

It's not like I don't still experience my patterns. I do. It's part of my humanness. It's part of my journey, which is ever unfolding and evolving. Some days it's easier than others. Some days I want to crawl into a hole. But the difference is that I now see this, observe it, and honor it.

As I begin to be more of this whole, complete, nonjudgmental observer, I experience some of the most incredible moments of trust, synchronicity, divine perfection, unlimited possibilities, and flow in my life. Becoming enough has offered me an opportunity to experience life from a place of more peace, ease, and joy than I ever did before. I am honored to share my journey of peeling back the layers to reveal more of my already perfect self.

The enough-ness in me honors the enough-ness in you,

Amanda

YOU ARE ALREADY WHAT YOU
ARE SEEKING TO BECOME. WHEN
YOU HAVE THIS INSIGHT, YOU
CAN STOP. STOPPING IS PEACE.
STOPPING IS HAPPINESS.

—THICH NHAT HANH

INTRODUCTION

As I was thinking about the title for this book and how I describe my journey, I kept coming back to the word "becoming."

Yet I felt that it somehow insinuated that I am not already that which I am becoming, which doesn't align with my belief that I am already whole and complete just the way I am. I kept looking for another word ... to no avail. So I decided to look up the definition, and, *voila!* This is it. This is what my—and, dare I say, your—journey is all about: beginning to *be* that which I already *am*.

This book is a story of becoming. Becoming that which I already am—which is "enough" (to the required degree or extent).

It takes you on a heroine's journey—my journey—to discovering the truth. After years and years of living in a story and under the impression that I am unlovable, unworthy, and lacking in some way, I travel to a land where all this is turned around and I am shown reality.

This book is about shining awareness on everything I learned along the way in the hopes that it serves as a light for you. As Saint Paul says, "Everything is shown up by being exposed to the light, and whatever is exposed to the light, itself becomes light." May this journey become a light for you.

This is what my heroine's journey is about. Rather than offering a solution, it offers a reflection of the human experience and predicament so that you might see it more clearly. It isn't a means to an end, unless you see the end as full recognition of your true essence and no longer living a lie. In which case, it's a means to the end of my belief that I am not enough. Not so that I can make more money, or travel more, or get a new job, or find a new partner, but rather so I can bring this illusion—this false belief—into the light and release it once and for all.

The journey begins in a very ordinary world—one with which you are probably quite familiar—full of fear, worry, guilt, shame, anxiety, depression, and disappointment. Experiences that turned into stories, which then became beliefs that I would spend the next three decades unraveling.

One day, I begin to notice this persistent nudge, feeling of discontent, dissatisfaction, dis-ease, but I can't quite put my finger on it. These stories or beliefs had become false rationale for which I need to defend and protect myself.

They had become armor that I had added, piece by piece, until there was no way the reality of who I am could be seen or felt. It's understandable—when you believe you are unlovable and all you want is to feel love, you will go to great lengths to go out on the hunt for it and protect yourself from getting hurt along the way, forgetting that the hunt wasn't necessary in the first place.

The journey to the already perfect self is a bit like traveling down the rabbit hole—without knowing exactly where it will lead, the further I go, the more I uncover. More than once I am caught off guard by what I find. I think for sure I know the answer and have it all figured out, only to be pleasantly (and sometimes uncomfortably) surprised.

The journey asks that I garner up the courage to accept my

soul's longing—to venture into the Land of Non-Judgment, to become enough and refrain from believing otherwise. I am only able to do this after years of hearing and ignoring it, all of which prepares me to be ready to accept it. As the mentors and teachers in my life offer me their reflections and understanding of truth, I receive the necessary courage and energy to accept the call fully and never look back.

Once I accept the summons to adventure, I am in for a ride of a lifetime. It takes me through the perils of perfectionism, doubt, and comparison. It asks that I lower my shield of judgment, which has been falsely protecting me my entire life.

As I open myself up to the vulnerability of being empty handed and exposed, I reveal heavenly treasures that have been waiting eagerly for me to claim. With courage, curiosity, and a sincere willingness, I find what is waiting for me on the other side of each perceived danger. Each fear reveals another deeper fear, until I get to the innermost one and discover what I have been searching for was within me all along.

I confront my fear of not being perfect head-on without my go-to defense of perfectionism. I learn what it feels like to move through the world without my shield, feeling things hit me for the first time—like making mistakes, saying the wrong thing, or flat out dropping the ball. What do I discover? That I'm still okay. It doesn't kill me.

Then I face my fear of uncertainty without my typical mask of self-doubt. I face all the discomfort that comes with feeling uncertain without equating it with something lacking within me. I no longer have the excuse of "I don't know," or "I'm not sure," or any other number of phrases that come out of my mouth when I'm feeling doubt.

Instead, I face the discomfort of the unknown with assuredness, confidence, and trust that goes deeper than anything I've ever known. And guess what? I'm still all right. I don't die.

Lastly, I face my fear of disconnection without my well-worn cloak of comparison. I learn how we are more alike than unalike. I come to terms with the fact that I am no better or worse—nor any more or less special—than anyone else. And, while I'm still alive, my ego starts to perish, little by little.

With all the treasures I unbury in the Land of Non-Judgment, I am ready to face my biggest fear of all. I am ready to stop hiding what I have tried to keep secret all these years. This journey teaches me that these false disguises cover up lies and that, ultimately, I'm not afraid of the lie, I'm afraid of the truth. By becoming enough, I realize that my True Self is greater than I could have ever imagined.

With my treasures in tow, I return home to the land I once knew, this time a person changed from the inside out. My external world may not have shifted, but my inner perspective certainly has. I no longer need to wear my armor of judgment to be loved, worthy, or even okay. I now see there is no right or wrong, good or bad—there just is. And I experience the freedom that comes with living from this knowing.

Yet the journey is not over. It has just begun.

This is the first part of my journey as I learn how to observe what is happening and see myself as other than my ego with all its doubts, fears, comparisons, and striving. I start to see that there is something much more constant and always free from danger that is noticing all this—the already perfect self.

PART 1
THE CALL

YOU DO NOT BECOME GOOD
BY TRYING TO BE GOOD, BUT
BY FINDING THE GOODNESS
THAT IS ALREADY WITHIN
YOU AND ALLOWING THAT
GOODNESS TO EMERGE.

—ECKHART TOLLE

CHAPTER 1

Opening the Door

Some of my earliest memories are of feeling left out, cast aside, unwanted. No. I wasn't abused or abandoned or mistreated. I was a healthy, well-loved, well-taken-care-of little girl. This is the power of story.

The story of a three-year-old in the bathtub crying as her siblings splash around laughing in the pool out back. A five-year-old being told, jokingly, by her siblings on the way to their grandparents' for Christmas that she is adopted. A seven-year-old waking up to get a drink of water and finding her family out in the kitchen having a pizza party without her. A lifetime of being called the "oopsie" baby.

These stories (which are not at all accurate but simply how my mind has chosen to remember them) quickly turned themselves into a deep wound I would carry with me for more than thirty years. These became the things I would point to, either consciously or subconsciously, as an example of how I am unlovable. The seed was planted— the seed of unworthiness, separation, and doubt—and I would spend more than thirty years doing whatever it takes to make sure I am good enough to be loved.

I can see the picture vividly. A little girl of about two years old with her cute, curled pigtails. Dark hair and dark eyes, shining brightly. Wearing her little blue and red polka-dotted dress. She is full of hope. Full of anticipation for what life will bring. Full of light and love for everything around her. She is whole and complete with her chubby little arms and legs, and her round, pink cheeks. She is love. She is fearless. She is limitless. She is enough.

This little girl grows up. Along the way, she begins to adopt stories as reality. She learns from others that there are limitations, things to fear, ways to behave, ways not to behave, what is lovable, and what is unlovable. She loses touch with that which she once was. She forgets who she is. She dims the light that was once in her eyes. For who is she to shine so brightly? She begins to doubt, compare, and strive. She starts to go through life looking to others to tell her how pretty she is, how smart she is, how good she is.

She no longer knows intuitively what Wordsworth so poetically expressed:

> *Our birth is but a sleep and a forgetting:*
> *The soul that rises with us, our life's star,*
> *Hath had elsewhere its setting,*
> *And cometh from afar:*
> *Not in entire forgetfulness,*
> *And not in utter nakedness,*
> *But trailing clouds of glory do we come,*
> *From God who is our home.*

At a very young age, I created a story that I was unwanted, unlovable, and not good enough. This tale is not unique. Each one of us has our own version of this story. Our own story that taught us how we are not enough. Our own experience of separation that created the first and deepest wound of feeling unloved. Many of us then spend years or an entire lifetime attempting to recover what we thought was lost, to repair what we thought was broken, and to take whatever precaution necessary to protect ourselves from ever feeling unloved again.

Most of us are inundated with self-help and self-improvement and think, "If I just find the missing piece or figure out my problem or join this class or get the certification or have the relationship or lose the weight or fix the neurosis, *then* I will be okay." But what we don't realize is that we are missing a *crucial* step that is keeping us in our loop of suffering. We are ignoring a truth that prevents us from ever feeling loved and reaching the level of joy and "okay-ness" we are seeking through all these other means.

My life was fairly ordinary. Sometimes I use the word "boring" to describe it; others might say "simple," as in not complicated. I grew up the youngest of four in a middle-class family in middle America. My three siblings and I were all raised by two parents who are still married to this day. I got good grades, excelled in extracurricular activities, went to college, got married, and made my way into a corporate job. I experienced no trauma or life-changing events like others I knew.

And I judged myself for this.

Why was I having such a hard time with life? I hadn't lost my brother to a tragic train accident. I wasn't battling a life-threatening disease. I didn't lose a parent at a young age, either through divorce or death. I wasn't beaten or abused or raised in an environment of addiction. What was wrong with me? Why was I suffering so much? Why couldn't I just figure it out?

My problems seemed so petty. Yet all I could do was think about how life was so difficult. Why couldn't it be easier? Why did it have to seem so hard? Obviously, I must be doing something wrong. I convinced myself the only way I would feel loved and good enough was if I did things "their way." Maybe not consciously but in everything I did, from striving to get good grades to saying "yes" to the man who proposed to me.

As a freshman in high school, I came home with straight A's on my report card anxious to receive adoration and praise from my parents. Instead, I would hear them say, "As long as you do your best, we're proud of you." I remember thinking, "How dare they! Don't they realize how important it is that I get straight A's? Don't they get that my best isn't good enough? Don't they know how much I am longing to hear them say, 'Wow, Amanda! That's amazing! You are so smart! You just proved how lovable you truly are!'?"

The funny thing is, I imagine most people would be *thrilled* to have parents say what mine said. Yet it wasn't enough for me. Spending my entire life believing I am not enough means that what others do or say is equally never enough. I didn't want to hear that all I had to do was do my best. After all, getting those straight A's was easy. I could definitely have worked harder. I could have spent more time studying. I could have learned the material better. I could have gone the extra mile, whatever the extra mile even means.

I chose not to hear what they were really saying: "Amanda, no matter what you do, we are proud of you; we will always love you." Instead I thought I needed to hear: "Amanda, by meeting our expectations via these external representations of success, you are worthy of our love."

My heart aches for that 15-year-old who didn't yet realize her own brilliance but needed to hear it from someone else or receive it through a letter on a report card. A girl who couldn't trust that her best truly was good enough, just like her parents said.

Even as a little kid, I tuned into the social directives to work harder, study more, and reach your full potential. I witnessed time after time how hard work pays off and that there is always room for improvement. I bought into this—hook, line, and sinker. I figured if I didn't try hard enough, I wasn't good enough.

> If I wasn't good enough, I wasn't lovable,
> and "good enough" needed to be damn
> well near perfect.

Recently, I have started labeling myself an "unwitting over-achiever." I know plenty of overachievers and, according to me, I am not one of *those people*. Those people do so much. They work so hard, achieve great feats, make lots of money, run successful businesses, volunteer, and serve on boards. They spend more time on their passions than I do. They work hard at achieving their dreams.

On the contrary, I feel like I am *never* doing enough. Even as I recount tales of my childhood I find myself diminishing all the activities I did well and eventually stopped doing. I minimize being a "good test-taker" or "not having to try hard at school." Time and time again, I find myself thinking if it came easily or if I was a "natural" at it, then I wasn't trying hard enough. As if my natural abilities—who I am at my core—simply aren't enough.

My standard of "enough" has been quite skewed my entire life. By the time I got to high school, I read self-help book after self-help book because I most certainly was in need of help. This went on for over a decade. I read about how we lie to ourselves, how not to sweat the small stuff, and how to be happy while not being perfect.

Still, I was doing something wrong. How hard did I have to try? How much more of myself did I need to fix? How many more books would I need to read before I was okay?

It would be many more years before I was offered relief, but this was the start of no return. These books (and everything else I was doing to "better myself") were the beginning of the unraveling, the beginning of receiving my call to adventure—the journey to becoming enough. The journey wasn't about trying harder, doing more, or being better; it was about revealing my true self by trusting I am enough.

Each of us hear this invitation to the journey at one point or another in our lives. It is the knowing that there is something else, something we have forgotten or put aside, something to rediscover. Many of us misinterpret this as the quest for something "more" or "better." This is how it started for me. I felt there was something lacking or missing in my life. I felt the need to improve things and believed that the only way to discover my true essence was by look-ing to others for the answers.

> The invitation came multiple times, not
> with a bang but a whimper. The true self
> has a way of being quiet and patient.

I experienced an uneasiness in my being that kept telling me there had to be another way—this couldn't be it. Another way that didn't require me trying harder or doing even more. I had tried that, to no avail. The adventure awaiting me was the discovery of my already whole and complete self. It was the journey to unlearn everything I had previously learned and adopted as truth.

The first time this soft voice tries to get my attention, I am 19 years old. A theater major in college, I spend the winter audi-tioning for acting conservatories around the country. I plan to take my future acting career to the next level (and receive my "enough-ness" from my auditors). One day in March, I receive what I have been waiting for—an acceptance letter from the American Academy of Dramatic Arts in New York City! Here I am, just about to complete my freshman year of college at a small liberal arts school in a small Midwest town, and I have the opportu-nity to pursue my dream of becoming a professional actor and move to the Big Apple.

After months of making plans and getting excited that my dream is becoming a reality, I find myself sitting at a local eatery with my best friend and making the hardest decision of my life. I choose to listen to my parents and mentors and deny the acceptance in order to finish college. Out of a desire to "do the right thing" and receive their blessing, I reject the call. I ignore that inner whisper that says, "I will be okay."

Instead, I listen to the fears that I won't make it, can't afford it, and will never find a "real" job if I don't get my college degree. I do what any "good girl" does and finishes college magna cum laude all while being engaged to get married.

A couple of years later, I receive the persistent nudge again. This time that soft, quiet voice within says, "You don't want to marry this man." I am brave enough to tell this to my father who, to my surprise, immediately gives me his blessing to call off the wedding. This time, it isn't *his* validation I want—it is the guests, my future husband, and my future in-laws that I desire to please. I allow the thoughts of "what will people think" and "what about the money we spent" to fill my mind.

I once again allow the fear of "doing the right thing" make the decision for me and walk me down the aisle. This was yet another rejection of that quiet summons to adventure—to trust that I am safe no matter what.

It is not until I am 24 years old, working as an actor and living in Oakland, California with Scott, my husband of three years, when the whisper gets a bit louder. "This marriage isn't working." This time the voice is too loud to ignore, even though I try. I spend months feeling split in two at the thought of getting a divorce. That isn't something someone like me does. It's not acceptable, certainly not in my family. The idea alone makes my stomach churn ... imagining how my family will react. What will my grandma say? Will my cousins ever speak to me again? Will I be the outcast of the family? Not to mention how his family will feel. The thought of what might happen and what people might think terrifies me.

So we try to make it work. I give it another chance. I deny my true knowing. For another few months, I weep and I feel like I am being torn apart from the inside out. I get angry with God and wonder where He is in all this. I pray and write and explore my feelings. To the best of my knowledge, I am the first of my entire extended family to end a marriage. Thoughts of letting people down, looking bad, being one of those "divorcees," hurting Scott run rampant.

After months of agonizing, I make my decision. I want a divorce. I feel as if I am dishonoring my husband, my family, and God all at the same time. But the knock at the door is too loud—I do what I trust is best for me no matter what others might think and no matter how "wrong" it might be.

The decision to get a divorce starts the unraveling of my need to seek my "enough-ness" from the external world—from my parents, my husband, an audience, a job. I trusted that quiet voice within for one of the first times in my life and did what I thought was best for me no matter the consequence. And guess what? I didn't die and no one else did either. I discovered that my imagination is far worse than reality when it comes to how people might respond. I opened the door to learning the greatest lesson of my life—I am always okay.

Yet, even though the door has been opened, I am not ready to walk through. I am not ready to let go of what I still believe to be true—that I am broken and need to be fixed. How in the world can I be all right when I don't like who I am? How can I be at peace with myself if I still have such a long way to go? How can I trust myself when there is still so much to improve?

For most of my life everything told me, "You're not okay the way you are. You're only good if you do things the right way. You need to be different/better/smarter/faster and try harder." So even though I listened once, there will be many more years of rejection before my soul's request is fully accepted. For now, I still see myself as imperfect and untrustworthy. I still need others to tell me what to do, how to live, and how good I am.

The following years serve as a training ground for me to experience what is ultimately holding me back and has me stuck in this loop. I continue to reject the call time and time again. I reject it looking for the "fix"—the thing that will make me good, whole, and complete—whether it be the next book, spiritual path, boyfriend, job, or diet. I reject it by continuing to seek approval and validation of my goodness, my enough-ness, from a voice that is not my own.

My primary way to distract myself from my soul's truth is with men and relationships, placing my worth and wholeness in what *he* thinks of me or how I perceive myself when I am with him. So I look for it from my boyfriend, the guy at the bar, or the guy online.

Before the ink is even dry on the divorce papers, I find my way into another partnership that will last nearly six years. I know immediately this guy is different. Early on in the relationship I learn that one of Daniel's favorite phrases is, "You're good in and of yourself." I desperately want to believe him. I admire him for seeing life this way. Yet the hair on the back of my neck bristles every time he says it. It is the very thing I am running away from, the last thing I want to hear. It goes against everything I have spent my entire life believing. I can't inherently be good; I've got to *kick, punch,* and *scream* my way to being good.

Daniel encourages me to find my worth and validation within. He doesn't want to give into my demands to be the one to validate me. Oftentimes, he flat out refuses. I see this as unkind and unloving, as if he doesn't care about me. I get upset and throw plates and tantrums when he "makes" me feel bad about myself or not good enough. I storm down the street in a huff, burst into tears, blame him for why I am so upset. He simply doesn't love me the way I want him to, which is a total setup for him since I don't yet love myself that way. Even though he sees me as "good in and of myself," I refuse to accept it.

While hiking together along the 2,200 miles of the Appalachian Trail, there are many times I refuse to adopt the way he sees me. On the third day of hiking, we are going down the rocks of Blood Mountain. There are little weathered "steps" all over its face, so you can go down many different ways. I go down very hesitantly and with great focus and concern.

When I reach the bottom, I turn around and watch Daniel just hop down a completely different way than I did. I get angry. I raise my voice and say in a very agitated tone, "If you're going to go down a different way than me, you should at least have the decency to tell me!" When it came to hiking, I looked at Daniel as more "in the know," as more right. So the fact that he went down another way was drawing attention to my being wrong. But there's no right way to step down from a stone ledge. I was down. I was right, too, but I couldn't see that I was already good with the choice I made.

I eventually end the relationship and keep resisting and searching for why I am the way I am and what I can do to fix it and make me more loving, more hard-working, less irritating, and less anxious. There is always something to improve, something to fix. I reject the call by picking up yet one more self-help book that has the answer for why I am highly sensitive, why I am a perfectionist, why I have a hard time committing to things, and what I can do about it.

It is no wonder I continue to reject the undertaking to trust myself and listen to that voice within. The beliefs that I have carried from a very young age serve me well and keep me safe, or so I think. For as long as I can remember, I feel enough when concealed behind my perfectionism, doubt, and comparison.

I have all these strategies that are well formed and, up until now, seemingly quite effective. When I do things just right, I am rewarded. When I second guess myself and do it the way they do it, I am rewarded. Why would I do it differently?

That is what we are up against when we hear the plea—the voice within that says, "There's got to be another way" ... the quiet voice that sounds like truth, but we are too afraid to follow it. We are up against a lot.

> We are up against having to stare
> our fear in the face without our
> layers of protection.

Still, through all my rejection over the course of these years, the appeal keeps at it. I get tired of the endless dating, or the endless drama of only feeling good enough when I have someone return my texts or tell me how pretty I am, or the endless seeking for what is wrong with me and how I can fix it.

I am ready for another way. I am guided to pick up books on Buddhism, nudged to seek out atheism and evolutionary biology. I stumble across more spiritually minded people and am gently guided to what will eventually bring me back to myself. I make deep friendships with women for the first time in my life. I start seeing myself as separate from the guy I date, or the job I have, or the city in which I live.

I begin to reveal how all my beliefs and strategies start from a place of judgment. Right versus wrong, good versus bad, needing to be more or less. None of it just *is*. In the months to follow, I have a lot of judgment to clear away before I am able to hear my soul's request again and, this time, accept it wholeheartedly.

For the first time in my life, it dawns on me that judgment is what is keeping me from accepting the charge of feeling enough ... the judgment I have of myself, of the world, and of others. Judgment that comes in the form of the shield of perfectionism, the mask of doubt, and the cloak of comparison.

THERE IS NOTHING EITHER
GOOD OR BAD, BUT
THINKING MAKES IT SO.

—SHAKESPEARE

CHAPTER 2

Meeting the Enemy

I have another story to tell. It's a story of a six-year-old girl standing in the kitchen, proudly helping her mother clean up after dinner one night.

She is placing all the dishes into the dishwasher, one by one, thinking what a good little helper she is. She completes her job and turns to her mother for loving approval and affirmation of a job well done. Her mother, a lovely woman who takes great pride in her home-making and problem-solving skills, smiles at her daughter and goes to the dishwasher where she promptly begins to rearrange things in an effort to teach her daughter the most effective way to load it. Sadly, while this may have taught the little girl how to utilize the space most effectively, it taught her something else—there is a "right" way to do things and she had just done it "wrong."

I was this little girl. Whether or not this actually happened, this is the story I choose to remember as an example of where I learned what it means to do things "right." It may sound silly that something as innocuous as loading a dishwasher could have had such an influence on my life, but when I think back to my first memories of learning right from wrong, this one comes to mind immediately. To this day, I can still feel the power of this story as I notice my stress levels begin to rise by the simple act of loading a dishwasher fearing that I might do it wrong.

For as long as I can remember, I have had a desire to do things the "right" way. This means I have lived most of my life in judgment. Judgment forms an opinion or a conclusion about everything—it is either "too much" or "not enough." There is a right and a wrong, good or bad, black or white. If I am not right, then I must be wrong. If I am not good, then I must be bad. If I am not more than enough, then I must be less than enough. It all boils down to this: if I am one and not the other, then I must be unlovable. The reason there is always something to fix is because I judge things as "right" or "wrong" and feel the need to right my wrongs. It never just is. This is why I wore a shield of judgment for most of my life—without one, I feared I would not be okay.

If I wasn't judging the hair on my arms, I was judging the outfit that girl was wearing. I judged myself for being too opinionated. I judged others for being too opinionated. I judged myself for being too lazy. I judged others for being too lazy. I judged myself for working too hard. You guessed it, I judged others for working too hard. *I even judged myself for being judgmental.*

In all these cases, someone wasn't doing it "right." It was me or them and, often times, it was both. Sometimes it was easier to judge myself; other times it was easier to judge them—it was one way of relieving myself from the weight of carrying around this shield, like letting air out of a balloon that is about to pop. I so desperately wanted to rid myself of this judgment and thought the only reason it existed was because someone was doing something wrong. I didn't realize I had it backwards. It's not as though I was judgmental because you were doing it wrong; rather, the reason I even perceived it as wrong was due to my judgment. So long as I view the world through the lens of right versus wrong, judgment begets judgment and prevents me from being with what *is*.

On my journey to get things "right," I enslaved myself to perfectionism, self-doubt, and comparison. I read countless books to find the answers. I signed up for endless emails and seminars and workshops. I wanted to be the perfect wife, the perfect friend, the perfect actor, the perfect meditator, the perfect writer. At the same time, I wanted you to be the perfect parent, the perfect boss, the perfect sibling, the perfect husband, the perfect mentor.

No pressure.

Through all this, I was looking to feel good enough. I thought *if* I shaved the hair off of my arms, *then* I would be pretty. *If* I was the perfect wife, *then* I would feel cherished. *If* I read all the self-help books, *then* I would no longer be broken. If *you* were the perfect partner, then *I* would be okay.

Each of us has our own incident that teaches us right from wrong and what it means to be perfect. Mine happened to be loading a dishwasher in order to please my mother. When I chose to interpret her rearranging the dishes as a sign of my doing it wrong, I internalized if I didn't do it right I was unlovable and, therefore, to be loved I must be perfect. And to be perfect meant always doing it right and never doing it wrong. Quite an extreme way to live. It crept into everything from how I loaded a dishwasher to the way I tied my shoes to how I composed an email to the way I practiced meditation.

I want to point out that the loading of the dishwasher is simply a symbol, an event that I chose to place meaning on and interpret in a certain way.

This is what we humans do, often when we are young and forming our ego's identity. In no way do I blame my mother for what she did or for my interpretation of the event. It's just an example of how we turn events into stories with meaning and then how those stories and meanings can affect the rest of our lives. That is, until we decide to question them, take responsibility for them, and, ultimately, transform them.

> Because of this pervasive belief that
> there is such a thing as right or wrong,
> perfectionism ruled my life.

This often meant that I ended up quitting sooner or starting way later than I would have liked. It also meant I would inevitably doubt myself and constantly look to others to see how I was doing—always looking outside for validation.

As soon as something was no longer easy for me to do "perfectly," I wanted to give up. It felt so much safer than continuing and risking doing it wrong, which terrified me. Equally, I would hem and haw and put things off out of fear that I would eventually reach the point of doing it wrong, which only meant one thing: failure. This paralyzed me. Failure was by far *way* worse than not doing anything at all.

I have had a love affair with perfectionism for most of my life.

There were things I loved about it and was exhilarated by, and things I hid and was ashamed by. I used it as an excuse for why I didn't take action, why I took so long to do something, and why I was so judgmental of others. I took great pride in it being the reason I have such a great attention to detail and am such a reliable employee. Many of us look at perfectionism and see it as having "positive" qualities (the ones to accentuate) and "negative" qualities (the ones to minimize or fix). I certainly did. It was my way of justifying this protective device. It wasn't until I redefined perfectionism altogether that I would be able to see how both the positive and negative qualities are "perfect" and inherent in who I am, and all of them are worthy of my acceptance. I no longer needed the label to hold me back or propel me forward.

The way I see it, we tend to get hung up on perfectionism in three ways: We believe we are inadequate and reach for a false sense of perfection because we forget that we are already perfect as we are; we paralyze ourselves thinking that "perfect" is how *we* think it should go (based on our limited and false understanding) as opposed to how it is *meant* to go; and we believe perfection is achieved by *doing* things a certain way as opposed to *being*.

So long as I carried around this shield of perfectionism, I would never feel enough, putting off the adventure awaiting me. I understand why I used it; it was the best tool I could find at the time and all I knew. As I got older, I started to look at my perfectionism for what it truly was: a shield that kept me from feeling loved and a weapon that kept me from loving others.

Whenever I held up my shield believing that I have to do things a certain way (and more times than not it wasn't good enough or done right), I kept myself from connecting to my true self and withholding love from who I am at my core. I experienced a barrage of insults and an inner dialogue full of critiques. "You didn't work hard enough on that," "You should have proofread that one more time," "You are such a slob!" Then, I projected those beliefs out to everyone else. Holding up my shield of perfectionism, I demanded that *they* do it a certain way and do it right. When anyone fell short of that, I withheld my love from them. The very thing I started using this shield for was the very thing it kept me from feeling—love and connection.

Another reason I postponed my adventure to becoming enough was because of my debilitating doubt. Doubt is another way fear and judgment parade around and keep us from trusting the voice within.

> We cannot trust ourselves so long as we live in judgment since it keeps us from simply observing what is.

Much like perfectionism, doubt springs from the dualistic belief that there is a this *or* that (as opposed to this *and* that), as if one choice is better than another and that there even *is* a good and bad—as if we are applying a valuation of sorts to our existence. Doubt keeps us stuck in the loop of "less than" and not enough.

My striving for perfection went hand in hand with my nagging self-doubt, a total lack of trust in my own knowing and my unique gifts. This doubt kept reminding me that there is always more to fix. I don't know enough, I'm not capable, worthy, or important enough. Who am I to trust myself? Am I working too much or not enough? Did I say too much or too little? Should I have married this person or gotten a divorce? Did I make a mistake?

Mistakes are born of judgment. If there is no right or wrong, there can be no mistakes—only gifts. Lots and lots of gifts. To doubt if what I did or did not do was a "mistake" requires judgment. Turning left instead of right is only a mistake if I believe turning left is wrong. Choosing this school, career, place to live, spouse, car, or meal is only a mistake if I see it as right or wrong versus a gift no matter what.

As humans, we like to have an answer—sending that message was "wrong" whereas not sending it would have been "right"—because not knowing feels uncomfortable.

> It is not the uncertainty that is
> keeping us from not feeling enough;
> it is our unwillingness to live with
> the uncertainty.

Should I do this or that? Should I buy this or that? Is this or that better? It's like watching a ping pong match ... for thirty years. Whether I spoke my mind or refrained from saying what I thought, doubt set in. Much like perfectionism, paralysis can be a result of doubt, keeping us from shining our light. I can think of so many times when my doubt would lead me to think through every possible scenario, without ever landing on a suitable option.

While seemingly harmless, ordering from a menu would often induce sweaty palms, an increased heart rate, and a deep sense of dread bordering on panic attack. I would scour the menu, reading each and every option, wavering between them, asking others what they were getting or thought I should get. I would be the last to order, delaying the inevitable, feeling the fear well up in my chest and apprehension tighten in my throat as I stated my decision to the server, disappointment washing over me the moment the words escaped my lips.

Undoubtedly, the next breath would be me saying, "I should have gotten *that*." And it didn't help when the meals arrived and somehow I always seemed to prefer what someone else had ordered, just proving how I, once again, made the wrong choice.

The mask of doubt not only colored how I reacted to my decisions, it also tainted how I saw myself. I doubted my enough-ness, but not in the way I would have suspected. It's not like I thought, "I'm not good enough to approach that guy" or "I probably won't get the role so why even bother?" Surprisingly, I went after a lot of stuff. I got leading roles. I got accepted into schools. I got the guy. My doubt did not keep me small by always paralyzing me; it kept me in check when my ego thought I was getting a little too big for my britches. "Who do you think you are?" it would ask in a snarky voice. "You're not talented enough to have this role. You're not pretty enough to keep this guy." Lying dormant beneath the cape of arrogance is more doubt, more fear.

If my perfectionism had me seeking validation of my goodness from those around me, my doubt made sure I would never accept it. It would sneak up on me afterward and say: "They're just saying that. They don't really mean it. You just got lucky. You'll still never be as good as she is."

This is where the cloak of comparison comes in, seeking outside validation—either by being "better" or "worse." If there is a right and a wrong and I am striving to do it right, I constantly look to others to determine my goodness. Using judgment as my measuring stick, I can immediately assess where I stand. Comparison offers me a false sense of security. Either I get to be "wrong" and avoid taking responsibility for my own truth or risk making my own "mistakes" by doing it your way, or I can feel safe in knowing that I am "right" and therefore better than you. Either way, I determine my goodness by those around me.

When comparing myself with others, I don't have to listen to my own inner voice. I don't have to trust myself. I get to offload my responsibility and trust *you*, and then I get to blame you when it doesn't work. It's not *my* fault I failed; I was just doing what *you* did. Comparison allows me to determine my enough-ness by focusing on what others have, do, wear, and look like, and then see how I measure up.

The cloak of comparison can be quite inconsistent. One day it has me thinking just how smart and frugal I am, because I don't spend endless hours shopping for clothes and material possessions that "don't matter." And the very next, it has me thinking just how stupid and destitute I am, because I don't have more money in the bank. Either way, I am not "enough." I am not accepting who I truly am. When we compare ourselves to others, we deny our equality as well as all the beautiful, authentic qualities we each possess.

Much of my perfectionism, self-doubt, and comparison stemmed from the false belief that I am lacking goodness, and the only way to achieve it is by *doing* or efforting. One of my favorite tools for understanding the human and spiritual condition is the Enneagram—a seemingly simple, yet subtly complex system to support the journey of self-discovery. It explains that there are nine personality types that describe human behavior. Each type has its own basic desire and fear that dictates how we operate in the world.

The journey for each type is to awaken to the realization that what we are seeking to receive "out there" is already "in here." For me, my primary belief is that I am not inherently good—that I am somehow broken and bad—and that I need to *do* something in order to *be* good. Get good grades, please my parents, excel at everything I do (and avoid anything that I am not naturally inclined toward), and do more, work harder, and constantly improve.

Ironically, this belief kept me from experiencing the one thing I thought I was lacking—my innate goodness. No matter how hard I tried or how much work I did, I was still never good enough. It was forever out of reach—an elusive idea that I could not seem to grab hold of. So I did what any sane person would do. I kept trying harder and doing more work to achieve it. That makes sense, right? If something doesn't work, just keep doing the same thing only harder this time!

This is why it wasn't easy to lay down my shield. I feared that without it I was open to attack. People might not like me or accept me. Ultimately, they will not love me. As a human, this is the worst fear we have. And, to some degree, I was correct. Until I could love and accept myself as intrinsically good, no one else could either.

For other types, it might be that you do not believe you are inherently loved or valuable or beautiful or wise or supported or free or peaceful or strong. These are what you think you are lacking and therefore pick up whatever shield or protective device you think you need in order to go into battle and reclaim it from the external world.

The mistake we keep making, however, is that the shield (or mask or cloak) does not open us up to experience that for which we are searching. It is a protective force; its whole purpose is to keep things from penetrating us. This is the opposite of what we are really going for—to receive more love and connection.

Not that this is actually found outside ourselves, but when we keep our shields up, we do not allow for what is already within us to reach others and be reflected back. As Saint Francis of Assisi says: "For it is in giving that we receive." We only receive from others a reflection of what we have already given, and this only happens when we lower our shields (or masks or cloaks).

While visiting my boyfriend's family for Christmas in Texas, I was standing in the bathroom thinking about these concepts. Oddly, inspiration loves to strike me while snugly contained within the four walls of a bathroom, oftentimes while standing in the shower when I can't write it down. On this particular day, an image of a shield pops into my awareness. I start to make this connection to how I have used perfectionism, doubt, and comparison to protect myself for so many years. Then, I make the connection of how I see others using the corporate ladder, alcohol, building a successful business, shopping, or accumulation of money to do the same thing. At the end of the day, whichever shield we choose, we are defending ourselves from feeling vulnerable to attack while on the hunt for what it is we seek. Here lies the paradox:

> We are invulnerable to attack because we already have within that which we seek without, but we can only discover this once we lay down the shield.

When I was in the early stages of writing this book, I didn't want to read anything about perfectionism, including Brené Brown's book on the topic, out of fear that it might fill my mind with someone else's experiences and conclusions. Still, I deeply respect her work and what she stands for, and I wanted to include a quote of hers in this book.

So I did what anyone in this day in age would do: I Googled "perfectionism quote Brené Brown." Lo and behold, this is the quote that the search engine returns to me: "Understanding the difference between healthy striving and perfectionism is critical to laying down the shield and picking up your life." Great minds, I suppose.

The lesson I keep learning each time I lay down my shield, remove my mask, and hang up my cloak is that I am already good. It's already within me and there is nothing I need to *do* in order to *be* good. Equally, I am inherently lovable and valuable and beautiful and wise and secure and free and peaceful and strong. Each of us is, and there is nothing we need to *do* to *be* these things. This is why it's safe to lay down our shields. Sure, at first it feels scary, vulnerable, open to attack. But it's only by doing so that we can learn the Truth, with a capital "T."

As we lower our shields, we begin to see all the things we desire reflected back to us time and time again in everyone we meet and everything we experience. This is our proof that it already exists within. If I didn't already know what love or peace or goodness felt like, I wouldn't be able to recognize it in another. If I didn't already have a reference point for beauty within, I wouldn't be able to perceive it in the flower.

My shield of judgment kept me under the illusion that without it I am not enough; it kept me from being who I truly am. While I might have thought it was keeping me safe, it was actually keeping me from experiencing what I truly desire.

My invitation is that we lay down our shields and learn to trust that what we are seeking is already within, and then give that to others more than ever before. When I began to lay down my shield of judgment, as heavy as it was, I began to transform the way I looked at perfectionism, doubt, and comparison, preparing myself to once and for all accept my ultimate quest.

My adventure was founded on learning to transform fear into love. I was unable to see myself as whole, complete, and worthy so long as I was afraid of what that would mean. I was unable to trust the all-knowing voice within so long as I feared the outcome. I was unable to realize my innate enough-ness without comparing myself with others so long as I was afraid of what it means to be connected with all things.

I had to stop trying to be perfect so others would love me and, instead, love myself. I had to stop seeking others' opinions and listen to my own inner wisdom. I had to stop comparing myself with what everyone else did or didn't do to feel special and, instead, see our sameness.

My journey to becoming enough meant I had to find the perfection within, trust myself, and see myself reflected back to me in everyone I see. And it wouldn't happen until I was ready.

THE BEST TIME TO PLANT A
TREE WAS 20 YEARS AGO. THE
SECOND BEST TIME IS NOW.

—CHINESE PROVERB

CHAPTER 3

Accepting the Call

I finally caved. Probably from pure exhaustion. I was fed up with not feeling enough, tired of constantly analyzing myself and seeing what needed to be worked on next.

I was done thinking that the only answer was found in doing more or trying harder. I was having brunch with a couple of friends in San Francisco, divulging some of my frustration. We launched into a fairly philosophical and spiritual conversation about our lives and how we were feeling. Eventually, my friend said, "Have you read *The Power of Now*?" It sounded vaguely familiar, but I had to admit I hadn't.

Something nudged me to order it immediately, and so I did. A few days later, I was talking with another friend of mine who was in town visiting her boyfriend. As it tends to happen with me, the conversation turned toward our views on life and what it all means. She said, "I just started reading this book. I think you'd love it. It's called *The Untethered Soul*." Again, this voice within said, "Get it. Now."

Within the month, I read both books, back to back, devouring the wisdom they contained. It felt like a huge breath of fresh air, as if a weight were lifted off of me. Both *The Power of Now* by Eckhart Tolle and *The Untethered Soul* by Michael A. Singer pointed to the power of awareness, of observing what is. These are not the only two books in the world, and certainly not the first, to speak about this.

I had heard about the importance of being present and aware of things plenty times before. Yet for some reason, as I flipped through these pages, underlining gem after gem, writing in the margins, it finally clicked.

> Not necessarily have the pleasure of meeting a yoda, I did. But recommended two great books by dear friends of mine, I was. The student was ready, so the teacher arrived.

We are each ready to hear the whisper in our own time. As *A Course in Miracles* says, "You will awaken to your own call, for the Call to awake is within you." It may look different or adhere to a different timeline, but we can't escape it; we each will awaken eventually. We each have our own "rock bottom"—a moment when we are energetically, spiritually, or physically forced to take a look at our life and examine how we are choosing to live. My rock bottom was not as deep as some, but it was deep enough.

I may not have been lying in a ditch or overdosing on poisons or in a near-death accident to wake up and accept the call. This is not to suggest that my awakening was "better" than someone else's. I say this because I think it's important to realize that it doesn't always come to that.

For some of us, we might not need to create a nightmare from which to awaken; being asleep is enough. It's enough to be fed up with things feeling kind of shitty at times, to walk around numb or disconnected from life. It's enough to say, "Why am I making things so hard? There has got to be another way." It's enough to say, "Just because I have a lot to be grateful for doesn't mean I can't awaken even more to the truth within."

My awakening was spurred by a much more subtle nudge. I simply got to the point where I was fed up—I had had enough of not being enough. I was done with the suffering and the struggle that, on some deep level, I knew I was creating. My life was "good" by so many people's standards. I had a boyfriend, a respectable job, and a respectable income. I lived in one of the greatest cities in the world, was healthy, beautiful, well-liked, creative. Why was I having such a hard time? Why was this not enough? How much more did I need to suffer?

This was my doorway into seeing the truth. My first pinprick of light. If my life was considered so "good," why was I choosing to suffer in this way? I was covering up this light with an obsession for fixing, perfecting, doubting, and comparing. Our portal to accepting our soul's work differs. Instead of alcoholism or workaholism, I chose perfectionism.

Judgment appears in each of these disguises. It doesn't matter whether we choose a pint of ice cream, a bottle of vodka, hours of screen time, or mentally spinning in circles to create our own suffering. Each of these distracts us from the truth that we are ultimately avoiding—*we are already enough.*

We might not at first recognize how difficult we are making things when we carry our shields of judgment and operate from a belief system that who we are is not enough. We might not recognize it because it seems so normal. Yet if we get quiet, even for a moment, and look around us, we begin to realize that it is not the natural way of things.

There is no judgment in nature.

Judgment is a human-made dis-ease. Nature simply observes. The sun doesn't discriminate which seed or tree it shines upon. Natural disasters don't seek revenge, they simply are. Seeds sprout or they don't. The wind blows or it doesn't. It simply is. It is our human-ness that judges it as good or bad, right or wrong.

When I read the words of Eckhart Tolle and Michael A. Singer, they spoke directly to this knowing. They reflected back to me what it means to simply observe what is and how common it is to create our own suffering when in judgment. It was exactly what I needed in that exact moment.

I learned something that I had not been ready to learn before. I was reminded of a whole other dimension, a whole other way of being. The very thing I had been looking for was reflected back to me in these books. I was ready to remember my true nature—which is nondiscriminatory and simply observes what is.

I knew I was ready and had had enough when the wisdom I was receiving finally made sense. It was like a lightbulb went on. It felt as though I was reading something that was written specifically for me or that I myself could have written. If this isn't the case, it just means we are not quite ready to receive the teaching being shared (or it isn't truth, at least not for us). Be patient. It will arrive and resonate when you are ready. It's a process of peeling away layer after layer of illusion that we have been wearing as armor for most of our lives.

I knew I was ready when I kept seeing patterns reemerge in my life. The same stuff kept happening to me. I felt limited in the same ways again and again. I felt confused and stuck. This is not how we are naturally designed to feel. These are indicators that we need to awaken to our call, to our already perfect self.

Life doesn't have to get so bad before this awakening can occur. Do not fool yourself into thinking, like I did, that my life isn't *that* bad. Notice if you have a belief deep down that you have not yet suffered *enough* or you are somehow addicted to your suffering. Until we are willing to observe that, we will continue to resist our soul's longing. If you are curious that there is possibly another way, listen to that voice. Let that pinprick of light be the portal for you to reveal your true self within. Allow yourself to be ready and willing.

Teachers come in all shapes and sizes. I have been blessed with numerous mentors who have shaped and guided me along this journey preparing me to be ready to receive my assignment. It would be dishonest or even ignorant of me to suggest that it was only one person or moment that changed the course of my life. Yet when I attempt to boil it down to "that moment" when things shifted for me, I point to these two books.

We can often look at different points in our lives as "the moment before" and "the moment after." Eckhart Tolle and Michael A. Singer served as the delineation between my life before—living under the illusion of judgment—and my life after—living in the reality of observing what is.

These books served as a pivotal point in my life. I do not suggest that these books will do the same for you. It is less about the teacher or the specific content and more about the readiness and willingness of the student. When we are ready, the teacher (in whatever form with whatever content) will arrive.

If I had read these books at a different point in my life, they may not have had the same impact. It is not so much about *which* mentors we meet as much as *when* they come into our lives and *how* they serve us that makes the greatest impact.

These two books appeared as a validation for me. They encouraged me to keep going by energizing me. While listening to a podcast one day, I heard how "aha" moments are not intended to be *the answer*, but rather serve as the energy needed to keep moving forward. That is what these books offered me—a slew of "aha" moments.

Our mentors are not teaching us anything new; they are simply reflecting back to us what we already know as fuel to keep going. As Eckhart Tolle reminds us, the teacher *and* the student create the teaching.

At first it might not feel like that, but that is what is happening. Even you reading this book is not teaching you anything you do not already know within. If something resonates with you, it means you already have some recognition of the truth. I am simply reflecting it back to you. The more you seek out mentors or the more times these gems of wisdom are reflected back to you, the more aware you will become of the knowing that resides within. We can only receive what we already have.

As I continued to be reminded of what my soul already knows through my mentors' reflections, the pinprick got bigger and bigger, offering me more and more courage to accept the perfect self already within. I would need this courage, because it was going to be one hell of a ride.

The acceptance was not the answer;
it was the invitation.

Acceptance was the energy I needed to continue on my journey. I still had a long road to travel and would need all the energy I could get, which was found in having these gems reflected back to me time and time again.

This is how mentors continue to support us on our journey. They serve as our reminders, our cheerleaders, our challengers. They offer us truth in whatever form we are ready and willing to accept. They reflect back to us where we are still blocking the light and refusing to accept our innate brilliance. They challenge us to go to deeper levels of awareness. They offer us a chance to observe how we perceive ourselves based on how we perceive them. When we are in judgment of another, it is because we are in judgment of ourselves. This means we still have more layers to peel back before we can fully reveal the unblemished soul within. Our mentors offer us this opportunity.

After Eckhart Tolle and Michael A. Singer, it was Byron Katie, Marianne Williamson, Wayne Dyer, Gay Hendricks, Thich Nhat Hanh, and numerous others who served as reflections. It was other spiritual texts that I read and explored. It was my soul sisters and mentors who I journeyed with in person and across space and time through the gift of technology. It was my family and friends who all serve as mirrors for me.

Soon, I would discover that every person in my life is my teacher, serving as a reflection, offering me the energy and courage to keep moving forward on this journey today and the next day and the day after that.

At first, hearing the whisper is not
always a conscious choice. Sometimes
our soul quietly guides us there.

You might notice that you get this "strange feeling" that you ought do something or go somewhere or talk to someone. These are clues to pay attention to as you awaken to your soul's longing.

For me, I paid attention to books my friends would recommend or hearing about the same thing multiple times in a row. Listening to the voice within is like a scavenger hunt of sorts, following a trail of breadcrumbs being laid out in front of you.

It wasn't as if I sat down one day and said, "Okay, I am ready to accept my call." There was nothing profound or prophetic about it. It was an acknowledgement, a quiet pact I made with my soul while sitting on my couch in my studio apartment in San Francisco. It was furiously underlining and highlighting words that were jumping out at me in the books I was reading. It was paying attention to the synchronicities of my life and taking one step at a time. It was an ongoing practice to hear a murmuring deep within and sometimes have the courage to listen to it.

I began to observe things instead of getting carried away by them. I started to get curious as opposed to critical. I started to redefine perfectionism, demystify doubt, and clarify comparison. I practiced saying "yes" when something felt in alignment and "no" when it didn't. I learned how to tell the two apart. I was gentle with myself. I continued to read books and listen to teachers who pointed to the same truth over and over again. I started to experience what they kept pointing to in my own life. This encouraged me to keep going.

Once I finally accepted what I was being asked to do, there would be layers upon layers of armor to remove. The armor doesn't magically disappear with a wave of a wand after becoming reacquainted with my soul. The reunion merely grants permission to explore and remove the pieces one by one. Finally, I am ready to accept the murmurings deep within.

It wasn't until I met mentors who reflected back to me what it truly means to observe what is that I was brave enough to let it be just that. By *being* more and *doing* less, I began to notice how I am already enough without "figuring it out" or trying harder. I still had friends, a job, a boyfriend, an apartment, and countless things to be grateful for without judging or *doing* more. I was still okay. This was a critical lesson for me to learn. If I can simply observe what *is* without trying to change it or improve it and still be at peace, then what else is possible?

Looking back, I now see how each moment of my life led me to meeting the mentors and listening to the murmurs the exact moment I did. The only reason it didn't happen sooner was because I wasn't yet ready. Each of us has our own unique timeline on our own unique journey. For some, your awakening may happen like a flash of lightning. For others, it may be a slower unlearning as you continue to receive the invitation over and over again. There is no one way to listen to the quiet whisper, no ideal time frame, no mistakes. Each step you take, each book you read, each person you meet, each relationship you have is exactly as it is meant to be, leading you to your mentors, your "aha" moments, your willing acceptance.

The way you allow the pinprick of light to expand and let light in is by observing yourself, paying attention, looking for the clues, finding the patterns, discovering the lessons, receiving the messages, and being comfortable being uncomfortable. While it is certain you will awaken, the path itself is ripe with uncertainty. It does not come with instructions. There is no map. The call invites you to embark on a journey with no pre-established paths, no prearranged rules, and certainly no certainty.

Once the quest has begun and the treasures discovered, the certainty you have been looking for is revealed—it has been with your perfect self the whole time. But not certainty as in, "I know the job I have will last forever," or "the relationship I am in will last forever," or "the experience I am having will last forever." That is a certainty based on permanence that does not exist. The type of certainty that is awaiting you on your journey is a deeper certainty. A Knowing, with a capital "K," that you are already perfect and there is nothing you can or cannot do to change that. A certainty that you are tended and always will be.

> Your soul's calling will start to make
> itself known in the recurring messages
> you receive.

There are different ways to get curious about your mission. It might be asking: What behaviors or circumstances continue to upset me? What is the thing I most look for outside of myself? What is the thing I most fear being without? Who am I being introduced to? Do they represent something I wish I had? What is that thing?

Are you being asked to reveal and accept the goodness you already have within? The love, value, beauty, wisdom, support, freedom, strength, or peace that already exists deep within you? This question is a great doorway to *being* more and *doing* less. What would happen if instead of *doing* something to create peace, you simply observe it deep inside and notice how you are still okay when things are chaotic? Or instead of *doing* something to receive love, you simply observe it deep inside and notice how you are still okay when someone rejects you?

> There is a reason we hear the same
> truths over and over again.

It's not because we're deaf or dumb or immune to growth; it's because we're being pointed to our life lesson. Even as we heed it, we will continue to learn the same lesson time and time again. It's like a corkscrew, each new turn being on the same path, just a new depth to explore, a new opportunity to recommit to accepting what is in each and every moment.

What I have come to terms with on my journey is there is no wrong answer. All of it is part of my evolution. All of it is for my highest good. I heeded the voice within when I was ready for another way—that simple. When I was ready to end my suffering, reveal the perfection within, and see things as they are and not how I want them or think they should be.

This is when I took all that I had learned and opened the door to the next stage of my journey. This is when I crossed over into a new way of being—a special world—where I chose to perceive things differently, observe as opposed to judge, and lay down my shields so I could remember I already possess that for which I am fighting.

Accepting the call doesn't happen only once. It happens every day. I recommit to my assignment moment by moment, for it is only in this moment that acceptance can occur. Acceptance is the beginning, not the end. It opens the door to a whole new world.

PART 2

THE ADVENTURE

THEREFORE, IF YOU ARE
SATISFIED THAT WHAT YOU
HAVE IS ENOUGH, YOU WILL
ALWAYS BE CONTENT!

—LAOZI

CHAPTER 4

Crossing the Threshold

After having worked for a large consulting firm for nearly four years, I was offered an opportunity to help market and sell an emotional intelligence training program to corporations across the United States.

I went from being a corporate ladder climber in a company of more than 200,000 employees to being the Director of Corporate Training in a company of three. I trusted the advice of a dear mentor of mine and the small voice within who said it was time to try something new, something more aligned with my gifts and my values.

While this new opportunity allowed me to prove that I am more capable than I think and validated my suspicion that corporate America is not a good fit for me, within a short period of time, it became quite obvious that it was not panning out to be quite what any of us had thought. Not anyone's fault; we simply were not fully aligned on the vision for my role and how I could best support the company.

Here I am, on the heels of reading those two books that served as such a pivotal moment for me, faced with a major life decision: quit a new job after only six months that wasn't quite panning out or stick with it as long as I could until I found something else.

Being armed with the truth and having had glimpses of it within, I take a path I wouldn't have chosen in the past. Still fearful of what might happen, I trust my inner knowing (reflected back to me by a coach I am working with at the time) and choose to be honest with my employer and step down from my position without having any Plan B in place.

Even though I am scared of the unknown (what will he say, how will he react, how will I pay my bills), I choose honoring my inner guidance and honesty. And the conversation couldn't have turned out better! I am immediately offered the gift of what happens when we stand in our knowing, trusting that who we are (and what we know and feel) is enough. My boss offers me a loving farewell party and thanks me for my contribution and directness. He honors my enoughness as a reflection of me honoring it first.

I cross the threshold and there is no turning back—I am entering a new world of listening to my soul's wisdom to guide me knowing whatever I do from this place, I will be okay. The months to follow offer me many more opportunities to see if I am truly committed to this new way of being. People ask me when I will get another "real job." Jobs present themselves to me, tempting me to go back to what feels safe and secure. My finances shift and instead of having a surplus, money is going out at a faster rate than it is coming in. Yet through each situation, I am respected when I stay true to myself and take the step that asks me to deepen into trusting the universe to support me.

When I decline the more secure and stable job opportunities, I am presented with divinely synchronous opportunities that are less stable though more in alignment with my gifts and desires. When bills are due, I receive money through more creative and nontraditional means "just in time." Sometimes that is through renting out my studio apartment to business travelers or tourists visiting San Francisco; other times it is through receiving a surprise, unsuspecting check from someone; and other times yet it is through a coaching client that seems to "come out of nowhere." When I am asked to take a step in faith, there is always something there to catch me.

> This is what I am committing to—an ongoing practice of putting one foot in front of the other knowing that I will always be okay, no matter what.

After stepping through the door into a whole new world, it looks a lot like it did before. I still have my same apartment, same partner, same friends, same issues, same dreams. The difference isn't my life situation; it is how I *perceive* my life situation. My tendencies and patterns don't magically disappear overnight. I still get triggered, feel pain and sadness, and don't know what I want to do with my life. Yet now I have a new way of being with this—I *observe* it. I don't take it so personally. I don't avoid it. I watch it with curiosity and compassion.

This Land of Observation offers me a new perception of the world and there is no unknowing this new way of being. I no longer need judgment to keep me safe. I begin to feel out what it means to move through life without this false protection. Instead of striving harder and doing more, I simply observe. I watch. I sit. I feel. I experience. I am.

Accepting who you truly are means unlearning everything you have learned up until this point in your life. It asks that you do what is uncomfortable. Comfort is safe. Comfort is what the ego craves. Discomfort and uncertainty mean you are removing the armor, piece by piece. It feels vulnerable at first, unlike what you're accustomed to, which means you're growing and finding your way back to who you truly are. The more discomfort you encounter and endure, the more you learn how you are truly invulnerable.

Time and time again I am invited to be okay with discomfort. This does not come easily to me. I have spent my whole life guarding myself from anything uncomfortable—be it physical dis-ease, emotional pain, or mental distress. I would go to great lengths to avoid any discomfort at all costs. People-pleasing, avoiding confrontation, limiting any physical risk or overexertion, saying "yes" when I meant "no," learning endless tools and skills that kept me "at peace" and feeling calm.

This new world invites me to live with ambiguity and step out of my comfort zone every single day, from not knowing if my apartment will rent out enough to cover my expenses, to asking for financial help, to being in a new relationship with open and direct communication. It asks me to feel things fully—pain and pleasure.

When you feel things fully, you start to notice that it moves through you or, perhaps, you move through it. You're finally able to release it and notice there is something far greater underneath waiting for you. We get to choose whether we sleep through life or are wide awake—and being wide awake means feeling the entire range of emotions, not going through life numb or cut off.

Of course, it feels more comfortable to go through life not feeling anything—this is why we spend nearly a trillion dollars on alcohol and pharmaceuticals each year in the United States alone. The reason we resist our feelings is because we judge certain feelings as "good" and others as "bad," and we want to avoid the "bad" feelings. When you no longer judge your feelings, you no longer need to resist them out of fear. Instead, you can acknowledge and feel them as they are.

The new world asks me time and time again to make a decision without "having it all figured out" or "knowing the answer." There is no luxury to weigh all options, do extensive research on what others think is best, or take into account each and every person's reaction. It's not that I now make impulsive decisions, though it sometimes feels that way. Rather, I'm learning to trust my intuition. I'm learning that my already perfect self, rather than my overly analytical and judgmental ego, is good at making decisions.

This means tuning in and listening for the answer in my body. Trusting when I hear a "Hell, yes!" and signing up for a year-long life coach training program without doing endless research or knowing exactly where it will lead me. Making plans and changing them, extending my trip to South America on a whim and experiencing the miracles of the universe when resources arrive to support me. Learning to find my voice to speak my truth even when it's uncomfortable or I fear "hurting people's feelings."

It asks that I redefine my definition of things like *debt, freedom* and *success*. I used to think success meant reaching some destination, achieving some result. *If* I earn a certain amount of money, *if* I get a certain job, *if* I lose the weight, *then* I am a success. This is no longer true for me. Success isn't measured in some "if, then" scenario; it's measured in *how* I show up to each scenario. Success is being fully connected to my true self, operating from that place, and bringing all that to what I am creating or doing.

> Success is realized when the true self is no longer kept hidden behind fears and limiting beliefs and is instead shared with others.

Of course, success often feeds into beliefs about freedom. *If* I am successful, *then* I can be free. It's easy to compartmentalize freedom—financial freedom, location freedom, freedom from time. But I have learned that freedom is freedom. And it isn't found in how much money is in my bank account, or whether or not I own a house, or whether or not I have a 9-to-5 job. Freedom is found in acknowledging and exercising the choice I have in each and every moment to decide how to observe and respond to my situation. It means being a conscious co-creator of my life as opposed to going through life on autopilot.

While many of us experience tremendous external freedoms, we are still prisoners to ourselves. When you hold onto fear and judgment, you are imprisoning yourself. When you hold onto "needing to know" or "figuring it out," you are imprisoning yourself. As global spiritual teacher and Zen master Thich Nhat Hahn wisely says, "Letting go gives us freedom, and freedom is the only condition for happiness."

While talking with a friend about what it means to me to be financially free, I said, "Making decisions based on my truth as opposed to my bank account." It surprised me when I realized that I already *am* financially free by that definition, even with debt and limited money coming in. Debt no longer holds me prisoner, because I *choose* not to perceive it that way any more. Debt simply means I paid for an experience with money lent to me by a company that I have not yet paid back.

As the apostle Paul taught in 2 Corinthians 8:14, it means that their plenty currently supplies what I need. It doesn't mean I am "bad" or irresponsible or incapable. It doesn't mean that I will be indebted for the rest of my life. A day will come—as it has many times before—when my plenty will supply what someone else needs.

Money comes and goes, just like everything else. Paul also wrote, "I know what it is to be in need, and I know what it is to have plenty. I have learned the secret of being content in any and every situation, whether well fed or hungry, whether living in plenty or in want." Notice that he didn't say, "Avoid debt at all costs! You must always have a surplus in your savings account!" For many of us, the fear of debt or not living in plenty restrains us from making decisions based on our true desires. There is freedom in non-judgment and observing the impermanence and seasons of all things.

Being a foreigner in this new land, I quickly learn that my greatest ally is my true self—my Observer. She never judges; she simply observes. She doesn't see things as right or wrong, good or bad but, rather, what is. There is nothing lacking or to be gained. There are no mistakes. The Observer sees the perfection in all things and has no reason to doubt or compare.

According to the Oxford Dictionary, to observe means "to notice or perceive something and register it as being significant," which is "sufficiently great or important to be worthy of attention." I interpret this to mean that when my true self observes, she notices each thing in each moment and considers it sufficient—*enough*.

My Observer serves as my inner guide by shining the light of nonjudgmental awareness on all things. Awareness can sometimes seem like the final stage, the ultimate goal, or the new world in which to live. If I am aware enough, I can reveal the perfect self within. Unfortunately, awareness alone can be a disguise the crafty, evolved ego wears. "Look how aware I am!" it proudly declares. "I get to point out all the patterns and beliefs you need to improve, fix, and do differently." Any and all judgment comes from the ego or false self. So long as I am still in judgment, my awareness simply points out my *mistakes* and where I am still doing it *wrong*.

The inner monologue of critique and judgment doesn't immediately stop in this new world. It still has its way with me, trying to pull me off my center and away from my truth. The voice inside my head continues to tell me how I am not doing enough or working hard enough, or I don't have what it takes. The voice seems to get louder as I pave my own path away from certainty and security, and I step blindly into trust and the unknown.

When you first step out of your
comfort zone and into the unknown,
your enemies will make themselves
even more prevalent.

The voice of judgment shouts at you to entice you back to the Land of Comfort—the certain and known—where the false self has taken by force its seat as ruler. Stepping into the Land of the Unknown, where the true self reigns supreme, means the ego needs to shout even louder to be heard. This is when more trust, more faith, and more willingness to be uncomfortable is required.

The voice of the ego will eventually quiet down as it realizes it's not getting a reaction of fear or judgment out of you as it once did. When you join forces with the true self and no longer desire the false protection of judgment, you are asked to transform your relationship with the ego.

At first when I became aware of my judgments, I did everything I could to try to rid myself of them. I started judging my judgments. They aren't okay, and I'm not okay to have them. I turned my judgments into my enemy. Once I realized judgment couldn't actually protect me from anything, I saw it as something to fight against. This was still based in fear. I felt vulnerable without my typical patterns and ways of protecting myself. I felt exposed, and I thought if I still had judgments, I must not be on the right path.

Judgment is simply a sign that the ego is fighting for its existence in this new world. So instead of trying to rid myself of my judgment, I start to befriend it. I start to be curious about why it's here and what it's doing to serve me. I start to *observe* it.

One day while hiking with a group of friends in the Marin Headlands of California, I notice my inner critic start going on and on about how everyone else is walking so fast and not taking their time to enjoy the hike. She just won't drop it. As I lag far behind everyone else, she keeps me company for a few minutes with her endless badgering. It's in this moment I feel a shift in our relationship occur. Instead of asking her to shut up or arguing with her, I ask her why she is saying all this. Why is this important for me to know? How is she trying to help me?

She replies without missing a beat, "Because I want you to know it's okay that you're taking your time and walking slower than everyone else and enjoying the hike. You're okay just the way you are." She wants me to know there is no need for me to feel bad for being slow or to feel as if I'm missing out on something not being with the rest of the group. She is trying to assure me I'm okay just the way I am. She points me to a deeper reality of what is. Because I no longer judge her, she is no longer my critic—she is a neutral bystander.

I now see how judgment isn't something to "fix" or fear—it's just trying to keep me safe. Of course, the true self doesn't need protection, because it is always okay and completely invulnerable, which is what this journey reveals. But the ego doesn't know this so it uses judgment (and other tactics) to try to protect you. Instead of defending your judgment or seeing it as the enemy, I suggest you examine your relationship with it by getting curious about what it has to say and why it's saying it. You may be surprised by what it tells you or what deeper truth it reveals.

Other so-called enemies I encounter along the way are simply reflections of where I still experience fear. Sometimes they show up as perfectionism, doubt, and comparison as I am asked to take more and more steps on this path with no map or clear picture of where I am heading. Other times, they come in the form of family, friends, and other mentors who reflect back to me the fears that I won't make it, can't afford it, and need to find a "real" job. Unlike the time in college, I now listen to that inner knowing that says, "I will be okay" and continue on my path into the unknown.

What I ultimately learn is there are no "enemies" in this new world; there are simply opportunities to deepen into my trust and knowing, and to resist the temptation to "play it safe," stay in my comfort zone, do what "makes sense," or do it "their way." This new world teaches me that I am no longer my greatest enemy; I am my greatest ally.

With this lesson, I have the courage to face something I have been avoiding for far too long. If I'm truly enough just the way I am, what in the world will I distract myself with anymore? Perfectionism, doubt, and comparison (along with all sorts of other false shields) are great at keeping me stuck in this space of thinking there is more I need to figure out, more I need to fix, more I need to protect myself against. All of a sudden, I can't distract myself with my suffering or hide anymore—I have to trust and observe and stand in my true knowing.

While visiting my brother in Florida, I receive an "aha" moment (a lightning bolt of energy to keep me moving forward on my journey). In a flash, I realize that I create my own suffering so as to avoid being "okay," because I don't know who I am without my struggle. This blows my mind! Accepting the fact that my true self is always okay and everyone else is, too, is new to me. I'm still accustomed to my false self calling all the shots as it has for the past thirty-some years. If I feel at peace and don't have to struggle, that means I'm living from my true self, revealing more of my wholeness and more of my power, which is totally unfamiliar (and slightly terrifying).

The question staring me in the face is,
"Who am I without my ego?"

It is my ego that is creating the struggle, trying desperately to find whatever it can to hold onto to feel important and necessary. Now that I have a glimpse of who I truly am—already perfectly divine—and no longer see my ego as an ally to depend on or enemy to fight, what is the point of it? The ego is terrified of me learning the answer to this question, because, once I accept it, there is no need for the ego to exist.

One night while watching *The Shift*, I experience a deep sense of relief. The film offers so many gifts, specifically how Wayne Dyer reminds me that there is no need to defend the ego because that is like defending something that doesn't exist.

Of course, I'm human, so my ego isn't going anywhere, but defending it is just another act of the ego. The pure, absolute self feels no need to either defend or refuse the false self, for both are just another sign of the ego's power. Simply noticing when the ego reacts to something or desires something is the way to disempower it. And the less power your ego has in your life, the less frustration and more compassion you will experience.

Some people say that we need the ego, it's important, without it we won't achieve things or keep ourselves safe. I see it differently. My ego keeps my ego safe. But my true self is fully capable of keeping me from harm's way. Why wouldn't it? Yes, my ego desires to keep my physical body safe because that is where it resides, but it has a much bigger agenda than that—it wants to keep *itself* safe by keeping me small and from shining my light too brightly.

Sometimes the ego will use my body as a ploy for keeping me safe having me think that if I do something that feels uncomfortable, I will die. But unless that something requires me to jump in front of a train, I probably won't. I'm learning that the ego has a lot to learn about death. But that is a whole other story.

The true self, on the other hand, desires to keep the *truth* safe, using your physical body as its vehicle and granting you the courage to step out of your comfort zone and do the seemingly impossible. You don't need the ego to keep you safe, unless by safe you mean comfortable, small, and denying your true essence.

As I explore this new relationship with my false self—seeing it as no longer necessary and realizing it's going to be sticking around for quite some time—I prepare to embark on a literal journey of a lifetime, traveling to Peru to participate in a sacred medicine journey.

The ancient tradition of Ayahuasca called to me many months prior. Grandmother Medicine, as the plant is referred to, started to make herself known to me through a comment here, a friend's experience there, and, finally, an invitation by a mentor of mine. I followed the trail of breadcrumbs, paying attention to the clues being laid out in front of me. The call to go on this journey is a clear "Hell, yes!" moment. I hear the answer and trust all will be well. The journey does not fail me. The gifts and lessons awaiting me are priceless.

During my first communion with the plant medicine, I undergo my official initiation of this new world. This is my test, and it feels like life or death, because it is—to my ego. Am I committed to this new way of being? Am I willing to let my ego (and all its devices) go?

Am I willing to die unto the false self in order to be reborn into the true self?

As I feel the medicinal cactus known as San Pedro, or Huachuma, course through my body, so much comes up for me. I learn that when I feel abandoned, it is not because I have been abandoned by others; they merely reflect back to me the pain of abandoning my true self. I abandon myself each time I give away my power to others by worrying what they will think or how they will react or by doing what they want even when it isn't in alignment.

On a sunny day in November, surrounded by the beautiful *apus* in Peru, I attend a funeral—a funeral for my false self. It's time to say goodbye to the fear, judgment, and false beliefs that are no longer serving me. As I lay her in the ground, I thank her for all she has done for me. How she kept me safe for so many years and did her best to keep me feeling loved and connected. Then, I release her and let her know I no longer need her. I lay her in the ground with gratitude and thanksgiving, feeling a sense of peace as I come to terms with who I truly am.

Unfortunately, this funeral was far more metaphorical than literal. My ego did not remain in her grave amidst the Peruvian mountains. She got right back on that plane with me. But, during the burial, I completed my initiation. In that moment, I fortified my commitment to turn the wheel over to my true self. However, this doesn't mean my ego won't still try to make its way into the driver's seat from time to time.

For many years I thought I was getting to know myself in order to "fix" myself. Now I see that it's not about fixing myself at all—it's about revealing more of who I truly am. Each layer serves as a doorway, getting me closer and closer to my true self. Each time I discover a new layer, I am opening a door and revealing the light of who I am at my essence.

Here I am, opening door after door with a whole new way of seeing the world with nonjudgmental awareness, and still I fall victim to fear. I watch, with love and compassion, my little threatened ego grab its shield of choice—perfectionism, doubt, comparison—and prepare for battle. Though this time, I know it's not doing it to keep *me* safe; it's trying to keep *itself* safe. It's doing everything it can to keep me from revealing even more of my light that puts it at risk of extinction. With this newfound knowledge, it's time for me to courageously lay down my shield and reveal the true perfection within.

This is why I'm on this journey and why I want to invite you to join me. It's through self-exploration that you discover the greatness already within you. It's a pathway to awakening to your already perfect self and sharing more of that with the world.

DEEP WITHIN YOU IS EVERYTHING
THAT IS PERFECT, READY TO
RADIATE THROUGH YOU AND
OUT INTO THE WORLD.

—A COURSE IN MIRACLES

CHAPTER 5

Redefining Perfection

Upon entering this Land of Non-Judgment, I was asked to confront my relationship with perfectionism face-to-face. When I took that first leap of faith and quit my job, I decided to go out and do something on my own.

I had no idea what it would be or how it would look. All I knew was that I wanted to share the truths and principles that I was learning with others. For many months, I was encouraged to start a blog. I hesitated. I put it off. I researched. I noticed how fearful I still was of doing it *wrong*. What if I used the wrong platform? What if I wrote about the wrong stuff? What if no one read it? What if it wasn't good enough?

These are the incessant questions you ask as a perfectionist. You think you are being wise and logical and doing your due diligence. In reality, you are stalling. You are avoiding the pain you might feel when you try something and it doesn't go as planned. You are keeping yourself safe by keeping yourself small. You are desperately trying to control what otherwise feels so out of control.

Learning to wield this new power of the intrinsically immaculate self meant confronting the fear without my go-to defense of perfectionism. It's by doing this courageously and willingly that I learn I no longer need its false protection to keep me safe, because there is ultimately nothing to protect me from. Yet with this comes a tension between false perfection and true perfection that needs to be resolved, a relearning that needs to happen. This relearning happens in stages; there are many doors to walk through with courage and curiosity.

I started out in the ordinary world by seeing perfectionism as my safety blanket. I feared I was inadequate and covered up my fear with pretenses—how I dressed, how I acted, what I said, what I did. I judged and paralyzed myself thinking that "perfect" is achieved by *doing* things a certain way as opposed to *being*. Eventually, I see a door with a sign on it that calls to me: "This way," it reads.

My curiosity is piqued and I move toward it with the encouragement of others. Through this door lies a brand-new world, full of possibility. Here I explore my perfectionism and start to see its duplicitous nature. I leave my shield behind and continue on my way barehanded and fully exposed. In an effort to protect myself from feeling so vulnerable, I begin to reject perfection, avoid it, and see it as the enemy.

As I move about this foreign, uncomfortable world and face rejection, failure, and making mistakes head-on without any protection, I begin to experience my innate invulnerability. At this point, a smaller, somewhat hidden door catches my eye. With my newfound confidence, I make my way over to it.

As it creaks open, stiff from being closed for so long, I am blinded by a light. As my eyes slowly adjust, I discover the very thing I thought my false perfection offered me and the very thing I then attempted to avoid. It is here where I reclaim my true perfection.

> Up until now, perfectionism had me
> stuck in this belief that I am not already
> perfect, whole, and complete.

There were days when it had me feel I *could* be perfect if I did things a certain way and other days when I would never be perfect no matter what. This is what the shield of perfectionism does—it covers up the reality of who you are and keeps you stuck in this pattern of seeking worth and value in other people's validation.

When I first realized this, I was anxious to no longer need it, to relinquish the weight of perfectionism. I left my bed unmade. I submitted articles without spending hours proofreading them. I showed up to meetings without preparing ahead of time. I arrived late to things. I relished a life without this paralyzing shield holding me back. Still, I didn't immediately celebrate my innate amazingness, running around proclaiming how perfect I am. It was quite the opposite. It felt super scary to renounce the shield. The truth of already being perfect is a whole lot scarier than the fear that I'm not.

At first, to defend myself against this new fear, I reject the entire notion. I choose to see perfection as something artificial we create to keep us stuck in this loop of aspiring for the unattainable or from doing anything at all. I no longer worry about doing things *perfectly* because there is no perfect to begin with! I judge the word as destructive and avoid using it.

Without the shield impairing my view, I can see the negative impacts that come from striving for false perfection. It bombards our society, marketing, bookshelves, conversations, you name it. It creates anxiety, stress, addiction, dis-ease. We pick up our shields and charge after this false sense of what it means to be perfect all the while running away from the true perfection within.

One day I was reading *The Surrender Experiment* and something shifted. In Michael A. Singer's inspirational account of living a life based on surrender, the word "perfect" is freely used throughout the book. At first, I was put off by it. Then, I paused and noticed how he was using it. It wasn't in the way I was accustomed to using or had used it for myself in the past. In that moment it struck me, "What if my definition no longer serves me? What if perfect doesn't mean something going exactly the way *I* want it to and living up to *my* standards, but, rather it is when something goes exactly as *it* is meant to?"

For a long time, I used to think my hair was perfect when it looked just the way I wanted it to look. Typically that meant like Meg Ryan's, which is hilarious considering how wildly different my hair is from hers! Or the audition was perfect because I got the exact role I wanted.

Once I learned to observe that nothing is an accident, I could release my need for things to be just how I want them to be. Just because the number of people at my workshop is different from what I want doesn't mean it isn't perfect—it is exactly what I need in order to learn an important lesson about perseverance or how I am always okay no matter what.

We never know how each
experience is preparing us for the
perfect unfolding of life.

This new perspective allowed me to no longer have the same recoiling reaction to the word. Now, I can see when you release your expectations, limitations, or control, everything occurs exactly as it is meant to be, which is perfect. It becomes a treasure hunt to discover the divine perfection in a flight getting delayed offering you more time with a loved one, or receiving the exact amount of money needed for an unexpected expense, or a trip getting canceled to find a larger life lesson awaiting you. For an instant gratification society, this may not be the most desirable working definition, because it might take time to see how a moment or an event is indeed perfect.

This requires a whole lot of trust in something larger than yourself—and releasing control. When I see perfection as things unfolding exactly as I plan or want, I am limited to things going a certain way and trying to control the outcome. Thing is, perfection goes far beyond your limited understanding and doesn't require your stamp of approval.

As I learn to notice and trust the completeness of the universe, I become aware of the perfection in all things. I no longer come from a place of contriving; I allow the divine perfection to take over and just be. It's easy to think that perfection is something achieved by *doing* things a certain way. However, if you are already perfect (which you are), then there is nothing you need to *do*. Perfection is experienced by *being* whole and complete. When I *am* perfect, that is a state of *being*. Observing the wholeness of all things is imperative to taking one step at a time with complete trust that everything will be okay.

To fully embrace my true perfection, I have to experience firsthand how I'm still okay even when I don't carry the false shield or pretend it doesn't exist. It's now clear I am no longer to run away from but, rather, toward the very thing I had been afraid of—*not* being perfect. Confronting this villain head-on without my typical defenses requires me to feel this fear fully. Any pain you feel points you to how resilient and invulnerable you truly are.

> If you are brave enough to feel the pain,
> you learn it can't ultimately hurt you.

This means that when something isn't perfect according to my standards or definition, I feel the pain of it. I feel the disappointment, the gut ache, the heartbreak. I feel the desire to do something about it, fix it, make it better. I feel the fear of coming up short. I feel all of it … and then notice how I am still okay. It's only by feeling it fully that I learn there is ultimately nothing to fear.

In this new world of non-judgment, facing my fear means making so-called mistakes, facing so-called failure, and feeling the nagging critic make a dig each and every time something doesn't go as planned or live up to my standards. Things seem to constantly "go wrong"—errors are endless, typos are commonplace. Time and time again things happen that test my resolve to observe my fear and remain in my truth, as opposed to giving into the temptation of false perfection.

You know that moment when you hit "Send" and then your gut sinks as you notice something now completely out of your control is on its way to inboxes everywhere with a glaring error? This happens to me a number of times in this new land. The ego, scrambling for its shield, screams, "Fix it! Make it right!" The fear comes bubbling up that if it isn't "right," I'm not safe, I'm not perfect, I'll be found out. Through all this, the voice deep within assuredly says, "It is what it is. Just surrender."

And guess what? I'm not rejected. No one gets mad at me. Let's be honest, no one probably even noticed, and if they did, that's fine. Even when something goes *wrong*, I don't fall apart. I give myself a pat on the back each time I pass the test. Each time I see a word misspelled, or a link I share not work properly, or a duplicate email go out to hundreds of people, or countless other ways it doesn't go how *I* want it to go, my true self observes it all without needing to fix it or get upset or figure it out. My relationship with my true essence is deepening.

Back in the ordinary world, the term "failure" terrified me. I avoided it like the plague. I didn't see it the way some people do— as something to embrace on the path to greatness. I saw it as utter defeat—if I fail, I would be seen as a total disappointment. But as I started to live from the seat of my true self, my relationship with failure also began to shift. Failure and perfection go together, like peanut butter and jelly. The more I am willing to accept my true perfection, the more I am willing to taste failure.

Thanks to two very inspirational women, I began to see failure in a new light. One day while listening to Elizabeth Gilbert and Brené Brown discuss creativity, my previously held beliefs about failure were called into question. They taught me that it isn't discipline that is going to get you to day two when you feel as if you failed on day one—it's self-love and forgiveness. You don't give up due to a lack of discipline or willpower; you stop because of shame.

This feeling of shame and failure is rooted in the belief that you are not good enough. Many of us believe that the secret to success and avoiding failure is to do more—work harder, push through, have more discipline. What I am learning is that the secret to success (whatever that means to you) and overcoming failure is to be more compassionate, self-loving, and forgiving, and then trust that you can do it again.

I have many chances to face failure in this new way and practice self-love when the program I launch doesn't sell to as many people as I want, or my article gets rejected, or I don't get the type of response I was hoping for with the launch of a book. In the world I grew up in, these would have been make-or-break moments and, more often than not, I would have chosen "break." I can still imagine the embarrassment and utter defeat that would rush through my body. I can still hear the inner critic say, "Well, that was a huge waste of time! Who are you kidding? Why do you even bother?"

Now, each of these moments is an opportunity for me to pause, practice more compassion, and then ask myself if I am willing to do it again. I don't believe the world needs more individuals who go out and do whatever it takes to avoid failure or give up when faced with it. I believe the world needs more people who observe those moments as opportunities to practice self-love and forgiveness and then go out and try again. Failure is an opportunity to notice how you are—and always will be—okay.

It's a little like learning to ride a bike to go through life knowing you are already perfect and that there is nothing you can or need to do in order to prove it. It can feel a little scary and unnatural. It takes practice. You're building a new muscle—or rather rehabilitating an old one that has atrophied after many years of not being used. It's all right to use your training wheels at first and "fake it 'til you make it."

> Embracing your perfection takes time
> and, like riding a bike, once you learn
> how, you never forget.

Even though it might be a little wobbly at first, there is such liberation that happens when you remove those training wheels and feel the wind in your hair as you cruise down the sidewalk for the first time.

Surrendering perfectionism takes courage, patience, and persistence, coming back to your true essence over and over again. It takes practice to listen to the quiet, confident voice of the true self underneath the loud, fearful ego. As I get more adept at listening to the subtler voice, I need to reexamine what *perfect* means and begin to see how I already am without having to do anything. I no longer see perfection as this thing weighing me down; I see it as my birthright and how all things operate.

Although words are far from ideal, they are the best things we have with which to communicate, even though they can be rather subjective and have multiple meanings. Still, they have incredible power over our thoughts and beliefs. This is why I appreciate going back to the source, the root, the definitions of words. As I explore this whole concept of perfectionism and how it shows up in my life, I want to know what I have been at first striving for and the next day rejecting—as if it were the last thing I wanted to associate myself with. What I find both surprises and comforts me.

According to the Oxford dictionary, the attributive definition of perfect (as in *the already perfect self*) is: "absolute; complete," which is the closest definition to the origin of the words "per" (through, completely) and "facere" (to make, do, perform). How many times do you hear or find yourself saying, "I'm not perfect; I'm only human" or "I'm perfectly imperfect"? This implies you are completely faulty. I much prefer "perfectly human," which doesn't mean I won't make errors in judgment or choices that are out of integrity from time to time. But this does not detract from my true perfection in anyway.

So long as you do, make, or perform something with your complete presence, it is perfect. So long as you allow the absolute unfolding of life to happen as it is meant to, it is perfect. So long as you see each moment as complete—by not carrying it with you into the next present moment—it is perfect. It is by attaching to the past or *not* doing, making, or performing that leaves it incomplete or imperfect.

> More often than not, it is your own perfectionism that keeps you from being perfect.

This new way of relating to perfection requires me to recognize my true self as complete, no matter what. If I am complete, there is nothing lacking, nothing to gain, nothing to strive for, nothing to fix. Perfection lies in the completeness. It is only when you choose to believe that something is incomplete that you can label it as imperfect. So long as you search for ways to "fix" yourself or fill the void using external means, you perpetuate the cycle.

I'll be honest, it took me a while to truly integrate this definition. It's one thing to say you are already perfect, but truly believing it is another thing altogether. Do you honestly know that if you say the "wrong" thing or fail at something you are still complete? Do you live your life based on the belief that perfection is not something to be achieved "out there" but is something that exists "in here"?

When this shifted for me, my entire life changed. I am no longer concerned if the font is just so or my hair is just right or the way I say something comes across correctly. I'm not afraid to try something and fail. Why? Because none of this changes the fact that I am absolutely complete. And guess what? Absolute means "not qualified or diminished in any way," which means there is no place for judgment when it comes to perfection. It also means "not subject to any limitation, unconditional; having unrestricted power." No wonder I rejected the notion of the already perfect self—this is a lot to swallow.

Even the definition that perfect is "free from any defect; faultless" now has a new meaning for me. Our true self is exactly this, all things are. There is no defect or fault in nature, in the divine.

The universe has no judgment.

The only reason I would resist this definition or see it as "unattainable" is because I am afraid to look at who I truly am and what this would mean.

Much like my relationship with my ego—once I learn to accept my true perfection, I no longer need to defend perfectionism as a trusted ally or reject it as an enemy. This is what it means to stand fearlessly in your power—facing your so-called enemies and seeing there is ultimately nothing to fear. Here you are free to be exactly who you are trusting that what you do is complete—which is always enough.

I experience true freedom when I lay down my shield and no longer worry that what I do isn't enough and start being who I truly am. As I start to live from this place of completeness, I take more risks, complete tasks faster, say the first thing that pops into my head, judge myself less, judge others less, try new things. I sometimes do nothing and am totally okay with it. I no longer worry how someone might react (or I worry a whole lot less). I show up fully present in whatever it is I'm doing and trust that it is perfect because I'm bringing all of me to it.

As I expose this treasure of inherent perfection, I begin to get a taste for what it means to be absolutely complete. I begin to taste the sweetness of being whole without limitation or conditions. As I savor this new way of being, my ego feels even more threatened than it did before. In self-defense, it begins to judge this in the hopes that I will limit myself and fear becoming too powerful. This is a whole new level of fear I encounter on the journey to becoming enough, which I am not quite ready to face. In the meantime, with the sweetness still lingering in my mouth, I prepare to confront the clever fear that parades around as doubt.

WHAT LIES BEHIND US AND
WHAT LIES BEFORE US ARE
TINY MATTERS COMPARED TO
WHAT LIES WITHIN US.

—RALPH WALDO EMERSON

CHAPTER 6

Living with Uncertainty

Here I am, exploring this new landscape of limitless possibilities, having adventures, revealing hidden treasures, and feeling pretty damn good about myself.

I'm learning to identify and listen to that true self within, slowly but surely. I've quit my job, placing trust in myself and the universe to take care of me. I'm leaning into the fear and moving forward despite it. I'm off and running ... or rather taking one step at a time. Sometimes with a bit of trepidation.

My whole life I have believed that not knowing is something to avoid at all costs. I have made "I don't know" mean I have no direction, no purpose, I will make a mistake, I will forever feel stuck and unhappy, I'm a fraud, I'm wasting my life. Quite the snowball effect! As you can imagine, not knowing has never felt good. With the hope to defeat ambiguity, I created a belief that there is one answer and it is right. If I can just figure it out, I won't have to face confusion anymore.

What I learned is that's not how it works ... uncertainty persists. So I continue to doubt myself, look for validation, seek answers from others. All this in an attempt to feel certain. If I *know* the answer or that I chose the *right* choice, then I can rest easy. In a weird way, doubt offers me relief from feeling uncertain even though doubt itself is a feeling of uncertainty. By expending energy wondering what I should do or should've done, I feel like I'm doing *something* to feel more sure about things. But as the wisdom in *A Course in Miracles* says, "Certainty does not require action."

The ego would have you believe that you could free yourself of any unpredictability if you just *do* more—analyze it, figure it out, ask more questions. The feeling of not knowing is so repulsive that many of us go to great lengths to protect ourselves from it, mainly through the distraction of incessant doubt. This doubt, which you may be familiar with, is born of the ego's judgment and the fear that uncertainty brings.

Somehow thinking that if you question yourself or others enough, you will find the certainty you are looking for and be okay, all the while keeping you from the knowing that already exists within. To keep you from catching on too quickly to its devious ploy, the ego fools you into teetering on the edge of "not knowing" in one moment and "knowing everything" the next.

Like perfectionism, these are two sides of the same coin—either you don't know anything and are "not enough," or you know it all and are "better than." Both of these are masks you wear to keep the truth hidden—that you have a much deeper knowing within that doesn't require any proof.

> This terrifies the false self. The thing that is even scarier than uncertainty is true certainty, complete *being.*

If I truly have the answers within, that means I am connected to something much larger than myself—call it God, Source, Universe, whatever. It means that I no longer get to look to others to validate my knowing or give me the answers. It means that I have to sit in the discomfort of "not knowing" on a mental level and lean into trusting a knowing that occurs at a soul level. It means I no longer have to ask the questions that have plagued me most of my life: Am I good enough? Did I say the right thing? Should I quit my job or stay? What should I *do?* This mask of doubt is stitched together based on the lack of confidence in who I *am*—doubting that I am already perfect.

In this new world full of opportunity, I no longer want to distract myself with doubt and doing, so I choose more trust and more being. I'm off to a great start and starting to get a little too big for my britches, and you know what that means: It's time for a larger pair of pants. This makes the false self nervous. What if I throw it out with my once-comfortable-and-now-too-tight pants?

In an attempt to protect itself, it reaches for its favorite mask and begins to doubt each and every thing in the hopes of concealing my inner wisdom. As I wobble around, learning to stand on my already perfect legs, I notice that persistent voice of doubt. My tendency is still to look outside myself for the answers, validation, and approval of my enough-ness.

I spend more than another full year stumbling around looking to others to tell me who I am before learning to go directly to the source: my true self. The difference now is that I'm learning how to play the role of the Observer and watch these tendencies lead me back to my*self.*

One day, while sitting outside Starbucks in sunny Los Angeles, the Observer apparently decides to take a vacation. As I sit down to write this book, which is pretty threatening to my ego's sense of who I am—certainly not an author or a channel for the divine—I run smack-dab into a wall of paralyzing doubt. This isn't the sort of worry like, "I wonder how this book will come into the world," or "I wonder how I'll make money to cover the expenses." The doubt that blindsides me is the kind that the ego just loves to sink its teeth into. It says, "Who do you think you are? What if you are wrong about this whole thing?" Notice the difference? The first kind asks *how*, the second questions my entire *being* and comes from a place of fear and judgment.

Plunking away on the keys of my laptop, I am allowing the first chapter to flow out of me when, in an instant, the entire message of my book is called into question. *What if it's not about being enough? What if that is yet one more way of playing small? What if I'm a total fraud?* It kicks my legs right out from under me. I stop writing for many months as I confront the fear and judgment and take a long, hard look at what is and isn't true.

Looking back at it now, I can see that the doubt that knocked me off my feet on a lovely January morning in Southern California wanted to keep me crammed nice and snug into my now-too-tight trousers. It wanted to keep me living under an illusion by having me doubt the truth of which I was getting a glimpse. Luckily, I didn't surrender to the fear. Instead, I stepped out into the darkness. It was like walking around in a dark room with my hands out in front of me to be sure I don't bump into anything.

Even though I'm learning to trust that there is nothing in this room that could harm me, it still feels scary to walk around in the dark.

> But it's not the darkness that I fear; it's
> the fact that I'm being asked to walk
> around putting my full trust in the light
> within to guide me.

What I begin to notice is that doubt isn't an enemy I'm asked to defeat; I'm called to explore my fear of uncertainty and, ultimately, my fear of knowing who I truly am.

As I feel more confident about who I am, my eyes begin to adjust and doubtfulness shifts. Instead of doubting if I am good enough, worthy, or capable, I attempt to answer the nagging question, "But *how?*" This stems from a sense that I need to "know it all." When I "need to know" and avoid ambiguity in this way, I am practicing a lack of trust.

> The thing is, as I journey through this
> new expansive world, I begin to see
> how I don't know it all nor do I need to,
> because everything unfolds perfectly.

I learn to accept the uncertainty. I no longer see it as an enemy; I see it as a reminder to practice more trust. Being in a dark room is not something to avoid; being comfortable not seeing what's in front of you is the key. As soon as you are okay with not knowing, you can release the ego's endless hemming and hawing that serve as a way to pretend you don't have a deeper knowing within.

This new world doesn't give me the answers; it asks me to be okay with not knowing.

Not knowing where my next paycheck will come from, how I will pay for my apartment, what will happen if I change my plans, where I will live next, if I am making the "right" choice, or if my boyfriend and I will stay together. But this intimidating new world doesn't leave me high and dry. It may not give me the answers, but it offers me a deeper knowing that everything is supporting me on my journey, time and time again. This is true knowing, which lives in harmony with the unknown.

Confronting the so-called enemy of not knowing without the go-to defense of doubt feels vulnerable and super uncomfortable. If you recall, I tend to avoid uncomfortable situations like the plague. Now, I'm faced with making decisions based on something I've never used before—my inner knowing—and no longer based on what you think or what the reviews say or knowing what will happen next. I look uncertainty in the face, muster up some courage, and say, "You don't scare me. Bring it on."

I say "yes" to opportunities without knowing *how* it will work out. I decide to stay an additional two weeks in South America with a friend of mine on a whim. I notice the uneasiness that comes with not knowing how I will pay for it or what will happen with my ticket or how my boyfriend will react. I feel the discomfort of not knowing these answers and stay anyway. I have the time of my life. My boyfriend is completely supportive. My apartment gets rented out. I go paragliding in Medellin. I swim with sea turtles and the Galápagos penguins.

I think you would agree, I'm okay despite the unpredictability.

This type of decision to change plans on a dime becomes more and more common in this liberating new world. Each time feels a little more comfortable as I continue to not know the *how*. Each time I feel a little more confident that everything will be okay.

I decide to relocate to Albany, New York for three months without knowing how I will cover the expense of my apartment while I'm gone. Upon landing in San Francisco with the decision to move in a few days' time, I turn on my phone to see an Airbnb request for my apartment during the time I plan to be in New York. This is the divine perfection of life. I say "yes" without knowing *how* and I am supported.

I continue to live on limited, nontraditional streams of income and go into debt. For some, this is sacrilegious. For me, it offers more opportunity to lean in and trust that everything will be okay—not in some flippant, shallow sort of way, but from a deep place within. I now see debt as a choice to use resources in service of my liberation.

From the outside, it might look like I'm making foolish choices and being irresponsible. I start to notice how, on the surface, things can look awfully similar to how they used to—but it's the inner peace and knowing that turns a once-confining cage into a liberating new world. Despite the discomfort of debt, I'm okay.

Perhaps one of the biggest decisions I make without having all the answers is choosing to leave San Francisco. For months, I was thinking it was time to leave. My boyfriend, Michael, and I are coming to the end of a three-month road trip (which was also a spur-of-the-moment decision that totally worked out), and I finally give my notice. Still, I have no clear answers as to where to go or if it's the *right* decision.

> Something I had learned is that you don't always need to feel absolute clarity before taking the next step; sometimes it is taking the next step that provides the clarity.

Michael and I pack up the studio apartment, getting rid of nearly everything we own except for what can fit in the back of our Toyota Corolla. While I know it's time to leave, I have no idea what's next. And not in some philosophical way, like feeling unsure about where our lives will take us or what is in store for us—in a very literal way. We load up the car, pull onto I-80 heading toward the Bay Bridge, look at each other and ask, "Which way?"

We have no plans. We don't know where we will stay that night (or in two weeks' time). We have no jobs lined up, no timeline. We have a few boxes and a deep knowing that we will be guided. We choose to head south. We could have gone north; it doesn't necessarily matter because either way we are held. We allow ourselves to be led and trust our soul's knowing as we take the next step, then the next, and then the next after that. That is all we had. That is all we *ever* have. And that is always enough.

Michael and I don't need to hem and haw and distract ourselves with doubt to feel safe; we move forward without knowing what's next. I learn to relax into the unknown by having faith that everything happens for a reason even if I don't *how* in this exact moment. This is part of learning to live in the flow and trust the true knowing within, uncovering the proof that I don't need to have all the answers and things still naturally unfold according to the divine order of the Universe. It's a little Nancy Drew-ish, pulling out the magnifying glass, and seeing if you can find the moments in your life that confirm this, as it does in mine time and time again.

Had I not gotten married and gone through a divorce, I wouldn't have the experience and insights I have to be where I am today writing this book. Had I not decided to relocate to Albany for three months, I wouldn't have been prompted to look into life coaching at the time I did, which guided me to my mentor and introduced me to many of the incredible people I know today, including my publisher. Had Michael and I not gone south, we wouldn't have ended up in Mexico and found our 90-pound furry soul mate on the beach.

I'm still in the midst of seeing the perfection of life unfold before my very eyes. The proof might be years down the line—I don't get to know the when or the how. This is part of the mystery that, as the theologian Paul Tillich suggests, is an element of faith. In addition, when you have faith in something larger than yourself (which, by the way, your true self is larger than your ego's sense of who you are), it requires you to doubt everything you have learned and seem to know up until now. It asks you to admit you don't know what anything means or what anything is for on a mental level. It requires you to release your grip on figuring it out and accept that you won't always have the answers or know what's next.

I grew up in a Christian household, though not overly traditional or dogmatic. My extended family, on the other hand, seemed more conservative in their beliefs. I had a push-pull relationship with faith. For many years, I saw religion as the institution with which I didn't always agree, filled with hypocrisy and causing war, hate crimes, and a lot of fear. None of this rang true for me. None of this felt like faith or God or love. So I rejected it and became an atheist. I wanted nothing to do with this sort of god.

Then, I started to learn about faith and God in a new way through books like *Wishes Fulfilled, The Impersonal Life,* and *A Course in Miracles.* I started to explore this idea that God is within me, God is me, I am God. Having been raised in a religious family, this thought felt blasphemous. How dare I suggest I am God! Yet this is your true essence—call it God, Source, Universe, Higher Power, Being. This is where your true knowing comes from.

For a long time, I thought doubt and faith couldn't coexist. If I truly believe, why am I living with such doubt? Since I couldn't reconcile this, I chose doubt over faith for many years. Finally, I realized that doubt doesn't keep me from experiencing faith, and faith wouldn't keep me from experiencing doubt. True certainty—in the form of a deep knowing that comes from Being—doesn't eliminate uncertainty on the cognitive level. As humans, we can't comprehend the expansiveness, limitlessness, and perfection of the universe. We can't possibly know from our human understanding *how* everything works. Yet this doesn't make the true knowing, or faith, any less real.

During my Ayahuasca journey in Peru, I received a very clear realization. In an instant, while lying on my back staring into the infinite sky, I experienced the paradox we are asked to embrace firsthand: *My false self knows nothing and my true self knows all, since she is created by the source of all divine knowing.*

There are different ways to explain knowing. As *A Course in Miracles* explains, there is perception and there is knowledge—perception being where most of us live and operate from, and knowledge being our God-given gift that is found deep within. When your knowing is based on knowledge and not just your perception, you know everything will be fine and work out for the best, and you are fully supported, loved, and valued. With this knowledge, you can trust and be at peace, no longer afraid of not knowing the how or when.

> Not knowing what's in front of me is no longer something to keep me from moving forward in a dark room.

It's no longer something I point to and say, "See? I *knew* I shouldn't have done that!" or "Since I don't know what will happen next, I better not even try." Doubt is no longer the reason *not* to do something; it means you're ready to go to the next level in trusting in something much larger than your paranoid little ego. It reflects back to you the truth that an element of mystery is a given when you place your faith in the divine light within.

This new way of being asks that I shift my fear-based beliefs and transform my relationship with them much like I did with perfectionism. Many of us resist the idea that we have the power of certainty within, because we believe it's profane to *know*. So we look outside ourselves, question the inner voice, and see knowing as a threat, because it is a threat to our ego. As Paul Tillich points out, there is an uncertainty in terms of not knowing *how* things will unfold or what it might look like, but there is certainty that it *will* and it will be okay. This is the treasure we each possess and many of us fear.

The ego wants to keep you as far away as possible from this treasure of realizing your innate knowing. This is the treasure you claim when you grow to a higher level of trust, confront your fear, and move forward in the dark without being able to see what is in front of you. The treasure awaiting you is an assuredness that goes with you wherever you go. A reassurance that guides you as you make decisions without being clear on the next ten steps ... or even the next three. The treasure is no longer attempting to discern the *one right* answer or questioning your decisions but instead trusting in the natural unfolding of life. It's possible to live a life that is based in trust as opposed to fear; it just takes a little practice and a willingness to surrender.

The treasure has been covered up by layers and layers of gunk that is keeping its light from shining through. Cleaning away the grime takes a willingness to get out the supplies and start scrubbing. You don't always know what you're going to find, which is why it feels scary at first. It's a little like pulling out a dusty, cobweb-covered chest from the depths of a dark, damp basement and not being too sure what exactly you might find upon opening it up—maybe a break-up letter from your first love, a shameful reminder of a wild night out, or perhaps something crawled in there and died, who knows?

You aren't sure what you will find so you choose to keep it locked away. But if you are brave enough to clean it off, removing the dust and the cobwebs, you reveal a bright, golden chest that is far more beautiful than you could have ever imagined, giving you more courage to keep cleaning and crack the lid open.

The journey is all about coming to
terms with the power of your divinity
by removing the many layers that
keep you from it.

As I start to wipe away the dirt and reveal my innate perfection and inner knowing—and experience how I am supported when I trust in that—I begin to experience this connection to something much larger than myself. I then extend this faith to others and to the entire universe. I start to see how we are all divine and inter-connected, which starts with being fully connected to my soul's knowing, my true self.

BE YOURSELF. EVERYONE
ELSE IS TAKEN.

—OSCAR WILDE

CHAPTER 7

Equalizing Comparison

I've already confessed that I've struggled to see myself as good enough. But here's the thing I like to keep tucked away even further: I also struggle with thinking I'm better than you.

If I'm not in some way "better than," I feel the pain of not being enough. This has been my story, and one I'm currently rewriting. This has been the way I've remained separate—from myself and from others. I fear that if I'm connected to you, I could never prove my worth; as if my worth, my enough-ness is found in segregation.

For as long as I can remember, I would walk into a room and immediately size up each and every person. I would see you make an error and secretly celebrate, determining myself better and, therefore, worthy. Sometimes I would even point it out or make sure you noticed how I *didn't* make a mistake, at least not one that big. Being better doesn't mean I never mess up—it just means I don't mess up as badly as you do.

While in a yoga class one day, our instructor reminded us how we are all enough—that we're not lacking or in need of anything else. We're whole and complete, in this very moment. Every day when I show up on my mat, I experience a different practice—sometimes I go deeper or fall out of a posture sooner than before. I'm constantly changing from moment to moment—my body, mind, emotions, thoughts. The temptation might be to compare my present self to a past or future version. I might think of how much I *used* to weigh or how much money I *could* make and think that's how much it should be *now*, as if my present self is somehow lacking.

Why do I spend so much time in this longing, this comparison, this desire to have more, be more, do more? Because I haven't yet come to terms with the truth—my absolute self is timeless and completely unchanging, which means that whatever I have been and will be, I already am. Being disconnected from this leads to judgment, and judgment keeps me from connecting with my true self. It's a vicious cycle. The real practice is to accept the version on the mat in this present moment.

> I can't believe I'm better if I don't in
> some way believe (or fear) that I'm
> less—one cannot exist without the other.

Becoming enough is my journey to bring myself back to a healthy level of relating to myself and others. It's a journey of realizing that I'm already whole and perfect and need not *prove* it anymore. I don't have to stand on a pedestal and shout it out for all to hear. I don't need to keep others below me to feel okay.

As I start to see and accept my own perfection, I'm able to extend that knowing to others, which means they are not less or better than me. We're all whole and complete. But for a very long time, I couldn't see it this way. If you did things that didn't match my understanding or seemed *wrong*, I would look at you and think, "Poor you," or "What is your problem?" Now, I'm learning to say, "That's interesting. Perhaps that works for you."

While writing this chapter, I noticed this deep-rooted belief that different is bad, different is wrong. I imagine I'm not the only one who sees it this way given the prevalence of hate crimes and war that plague humanity. Xenophobia is part of our evolutionary biology, after all, protecting us from potential enemies, ensuring our survival. What we don't know is threatening.

Typically, when you compare, you differentiate. This leads to uncertainty so you attempt to protect yourself. You can either see yourself as wrong and choose their way through imitation, becoming a part of their group; you can see them as wrong and rebel, maintaining your individuality; or you can see them as wrong and attempt to control them by forcing them to follow your way (and killing them off if they don't).

What I finally realized is that comparison in and of itself is neutral. It simply notices the similarities or dissimilarities between things, which doesn't imply bad or wrong. It's only when I come from a place of judgment that I feel the need to protect myself with the cloak of comparison. This leads to separation—the opposite thing I'm going for.

The cloak serves as a false sense of connection by comparing everything on a surface level, while covering up the fact that we *are* ultimately connected, cut of the same cloth. It's not our differences that truly scare us; it's the truth we are all one that is terrifying to the ego.

The ego thrives on separation and feeling different than others. If I remove the cloak and compare in a healthy nonjudgmental way, I have to accept that we are far more similar than I want to believe and see surface-level differences as non-threatening. I have to accept that those things I see in you are also in me—wanted or unwanted. My false self no longer gets to parade around saying, "See, I'm so superior to you, I'm far more powerful."

Equally, it doesn't get to say, "See, I'm so much worse off than you, I'm not nearly as powerful." I no longer get to think that power is found in separation and difference, but rather in connection and integration. If we are equal that means I don't get to be especially amazing or especially tragic.

On a sunny day in Peru while feeling the wisdom of San Pedro course through my body, I begin to explore the house of my shaman, which is supposed to be off-limits during ceremony. When he finds me, instead of asking me to leave, he offers to give me a tour. Immediately, I light up and think, "I am so special." As quickly as that thought occurs, I want to reject it as unkind or thoughtless of others. Then Grandmother Medicine reminds me that I *am* special—we all are— and there is nothing bad or wrong for believing this. The separation occurs when I think I am the *only* one who is special or am more special than you. I hate to break it to you, but you are just as special as I am.

The ego loves to fool me into thinking I'm not safe if I see the interconnection and equality of all things, so it uses judgment to differentiate and cause more separation. As an actor, I would consistently walk into an audition and, within moments, size up each and every person, comparing myself to each one and critiquing who falls where. If we're one, then I don't know where I rank in the hierarchy. If I'm not on the top, then I'm dinner—I don't get the role. I was trying to protect myself. It took years before it would occur to me that perhaps you were simply a better fit for the part and it had nothing to do with my personal character or ability—or survival.

When you remove the cloak, you start to see how everything around you—including the magnificent sunset or the awe-inspiring mountain top—is a reflection of your inner perfect self. As you begin to experience this divine interconnectedness, you no longer fear losing yourself nor do you need a false cloak of comparison to keep yourself feeling safe and connected to all things.

> Awakening to the knowledge that we
> are all connected, all cut of the same
> cloth, is the death of the ego.

The ego's entire purpose is to separate through illusion. If I see us as one, we must be equal. If we are equal, my ego no longer has anything to hang its hat on ... or should I say, cloak? Without my cloak, I must accept that there is something much larger by which we are all connected.

I must be willing to extend grace and compassion to myself and others, which is often the last thing I want to do. I must be willing to release judgment and simply observe you for who you truly are. I no longer get to take the easy way out and look to you to tell me what to do. While uncomfortable and awkward at first, much like going on a first date, realizing the truth of interconnectedness eventually feels like sitting down with a long-lost friend over a cup of coffee, staring into her eyes, sharing your deepest secrets, and feeling seen, loved, and safe in her presence.

Many of us have been socialized our entire lives to trust that so-and-so knows best. First, it's parents, then teachers, mentors, friends, the expert, the person who is offering a webinar ... the list goes on and on. Starting at a very early age, I was discouraged—if not flat out restricted—from listening to my inner knowing. I was told to stop crying, how I should feel, when to eat, what to eat, when to go to bed, how to spend my time, what hobbies to enjoy, how to spend my money, what job to get, what relationship is best. I was told I "have to" or "should" even when it didn't feel right.

By the time I was 19 years old, my soul's knowing told me to move to New York, that I would be okay. But, by this point, I had been conditioned to listen to everyone *other* than my inner wisdom. *They* knew what was best.

Once that inner voice gets drowned out, before you know it you're looking to everyone *but* yourself for your answers, worth, okay-ness. We live in a self-help age where we are inundated with the "top ten secrets" or a "how-to" on any topic you could ever imagine. We're told that to be successful you just need to follow "these three steps." We're offered up expert after expert who supposedly has the answer. Frustrated and exhausted, you attempt to find your own way amidst all this noise.

I'm not suggesting you stop acquiring knowledge or skills. This is part of the journey. I'm done thinking that who I am isn't enough, but I'm certainly not done learning! I still look to others, but now I do it with a different intention. Instead of seeking out teachings to give me *the* answer or to offer me something that I'm missing, I now see them pointing me back to what I already know to be true within. Sometimes this is easier said than done.

I have done a great job over the course of my life to cover up my inner knowing with other people's opinions, obligations, childhood wounds, limiting beliefs, and dependencies. The journey invites me to clear that all away. Revealing your inner wisdom is sometimes uncomfortable as it asks you to do things that you aren't always willing to do, like bite your tongue, move out of your apartment, quit your job, write the book, leave the relationship, stick it out. It asks you to step outside your comfort zone and experiment with new ways of being.

The times in my life I find myself picking up my cloak of comparison is when I'm least trusting of what it is I'm doing. The more I'm living in doubt, the more I use the cloak to keep me safe. However, when I'm feeling connected to my inner knowing, I have no need to compare myself to past or future versions or see how others are doing it.

As a path-paver in this uncharted world, I have many opportunities to doubt myself. I'm asked to take my connection to my inner GPS to a whole new level. I'm bombarded with three steps to success and hundreds of experts who tell me how to promote my book, make six figures, or lose ten pounds.

There is a formula for pretty much everything. If I follow this step-by-step approach, my life can look just like yours. My ego reaches for its cloak, all in an attempt to feel more certain. I use other people as a gauge, a measure, a yardstick of sorts. I think that if it worked for them it must work for me. And if it looks different, I must be doing it *wrong*. The mask of doubt and cloak of comparison go hand in hand. The more I doubt my true self, the more I seek my truth in someone else.

One day, I was on social media and saw an ad for this incredibly successful woman in the online world. I immediately felt that sinking feeling in my stomach and the spiraling of doubts and insecurities, wondering if I need to learn more about online marketing and teach people how to do *that*, because that seems to make money. Then, I paused. I noticed these thoughts and feelings swirling all around me, and I recommitted to my soul's work in the world and how I want to serve.

This can feel difficult sometimes when there are so many incredibly successful and smart people all around you. It can be all too easy to get in this place of comparison and thoughts like, "I need to do things more like them."

> It's a lack of connection and trust in your true self that leads to imitation.

A million people all starting businesses, driving cars, living in houses, having relationships, wearing clothes that all look the same. Before you know it, you are no longer focusing on what matters most to you, what lights you up, what resonates with your soul's longing, what's already "in here."

As I first learn how to navigate this new authentic world, I find myself doing this time and time again. On one such occasion, I have this realization that when I copy someone else and do it "her way," I'm covering up a fear that I have nothing original to offer. Of course, my infinite self knows this isn't true. When I'm authentically true to myself, I do things in an original way, which means there is no copy or imitation even if it's similar to someone else. *This* is what your authentic self is—real, existing from the beginning, genuine.

It's the limitlessness that is terrifying to the ego, because it's in the eternal, the infinite where the ego dies. If I no longer look to others to "show me the way" or "tell me what to do," I have endless possibilities. It's up to the divine navigator within to show me the way. When I take your word for it, do it your way, follow your ten-step formula, and ignore my authentic voice, I'm offloading my responsibility.

It requires radical self-responsibility to be authentic, to stand in my true knowing. It requires me to get clear on what I truly desire, to wipe away the fog and take a good, long look in the mirror at the already perfect self. It requires I show up consciously as a co-creator of my life, as opposed to running on autopilot doing what others tell me to do or rebelling out of spite.

When I initially left my cloak hanging in the closet, I found that I had to get to know my true desires for one of the first times in my life. At first, if mentors or experts said to use my social media platform to connect with my audience and build my tribe, I followed suit. Because it wasn't aligned with my true self, it didn't work. After realizing this, I was told that to expand my reach and sell my services I needed to post in a certain number of groups a day. I refused.

It felt completely inauthentic to me (and I didn't want to do it just because I was supposed to). This isn't to say people don't have great success connecting with others on social media; it simply highlights that just because others do something doesn't mean you need to or will have the same experience if you do.

For so long, I had chosen conformity and imitation that I needed to distance myself from that in order to know what was true for me. After learning to say "no," I learned to discern what felt true to me even if others were doing it. I didn't need to be stubborn just for the sake of being stubborn. Even though a lot of people launch radio shows—and some as a strategic move for their business—I noticed how aligned it was to my soul, so I did it. And not as a business tactic—but because it completely lights me up.

One beautiful fall Wednesday in San Francisco, I found myself lying in the park for hours not doing anything. I was reconnecting with my beloved Michael after having been apart for nearly two months. I noticed all these other people in the park in the middle of the day and thought, *I wonder if any of them are also thinking that they are wasting time and should be doing something else.*

I started to compare my experience with theirs. I was looking for them to validate my enough-ness. If they were confident in their knowing that this was a perfectly acceptable way to spend one's time, then I could feel good also seeing it that way. Immediately, I heard this voice within me say, "It doesn't matter. They are each on their own journey, and you are on yours." This is what it's like to be connected with my inner wisdom and no longer need to look to others for validation.

This journey is a bit like a set of Russian nesting dolls. It starts with the outermost doll covering up my fear of not being worthy, so I parade around as better or less than, creating separation.

Then, the next doll reveals my fear that I'm not connected (to myself or others), so I go around trying to be more like you thinking this will fill that hole. I can then compare how I measure up and either feel superior or inferior.

The next doll represents my deeper fear of true connection—true oneness—so I rebel or shun you. I refuse to see us as similar, so I do what I can to feel separate and different, unique, or special. Once I see the true fear for what it is, I reveal the final doll that represents how we are all interconnected and I no longer need to conform or rebel since I've now reached the reality of who we are and see us as one. It doesn't matter if, on the surface, I'm like you or not, or do things the way you do them or not—neither is good nor bad, neither validates my worth or goodness, neither makes us any more or less equal.

The fact is, what I see in you is already living within me—the brilliance, success, joy, happiness, sadness, sorrow, anger, self-destruction, dis-ease. It's all in *here* because we all come from the same source. This is why there is no real separation. In those moments when I compare and see myself as "less than," I'm choosing to forget that the brilliance, wisdom, and strength I perceive in you is lying dormant within. When I see myself as "better than," I'm choosing to forget that I, too, feel pain, addiction, separation, and disconnection.

All those things you hate about other people, the things that irritate you, the things that you find yourself getting so upset about—look more closely. You might be surprised to find those things are in your very own backyard, parts of yourself that you are disowning. You don't need to strive to keep those unwanted parts hidden no matter how repulsive, off-putting, or daunting they may seem. All it does is manifest weeds that prevent your flowers from thriving.

Rather, you need to acknowledge them, learn to cultivate them, and grow compassion for them. You might find they won't take over in a negative way if you add them to your compost and use them as fertilizer.

My shaman in Peru introduced me to a new perspective of compassion based on the teachings of Pema Chödrön—allowing someone's (including my) experience to be what it is. She says, "Having compassion starts and ends with having compassion for all those unwanted parts of ourselves. The healing comes from letting there be room for all this to happen: room for grief, for relief, for misery, for joy." So long as we separate out parts of ourselves as *good* and *bad*, we separate ourselves from others. We remain disconnected.

The practice is to see our unity—within ourselves and with others. Like Chödrön says, "Compassion is not a relationship between the healer and the wounded. It's a relationship between equals. Only when we know our own darkness well can we be present with the darkness of others. Compassion becomes real when we recognize our shared humanity."

> Our shared humanity includes both the
> unwanted and wanted parts.

All those things you admire about other people are also in your own backyard, just waiting to push up through the soil and blossom into beautiful flowers. Once I start to notice how your magnificence is a reflection of what is within me, my entire world shifts. I no longer feel jealous or envious. I see you as a representation of what's possible and already living within me at this very moment.

This is the gift of being one. We are limitless, which means there is an infinite amount of success to be had, joy to be felt, happiness to be experienced, and goodness to be expressed. It's our lack mentality and forgetting our true nature—that we are equally as deserving—that breeds jealousy and envy.

Like all the other disguises of judgment, when you use comparison as a false protection, you don't get a chance to reveal to yourself and the world that your enough-ness is enough—whether that comes in a straight, gay, black, white, male, female, addicted, thin, or full-figured package.

There is no need to compare and put some above or below others. Who we truly are is the same. Enough is enough is enough, and the "enough" within is far beyond what you could ever imagine. It's not through your cloak of comparison that you will discover your worthiness; it's by seeing yourself as whole and equal with *all* things that will reveal your magnitude.

I see my essence and power reflected back to me through you. When I learn of your success, your strength, your perspective, I now see what is living within me. I get a clearer picture of my own limitlessness and potential. Instead of going into a spiral of how to be more like *you*, I ask how I can be more of *me*.

During a personal development program, I sat in circle with a few people and heard them share how they see themselves, the gifts they have to offer, the essence of who they are. In that moment, I experienced deep emotion move through my body. I asked my facilitator what was happening, and he shared with me that I was experiencing the truth of seeing my own inner essence reflected back to me by each person. What I heard, felt, and witnessed was so beautiful that it brought tears to my eyes. This is what happens when we are willing to experience our true connection.

Comparison isn't something to fix or defeat.

When you choose observation over judgment, it offers you an opportunity to reconnect with your true self and see your interconnectedness with *all* things. Through this lens, comparison now offers us a way of observing our surface-level differences nonjudgmentally and the similar qualities we share at our core with joy and greater compassion. I no longer see myself as "different" when I compare; I now see the divine sameness we share.

As Thich Nhat Hanh explains in *You Are Here*, "Look into yourself and you will see that you are not a separate entity. ... You carry in you the whole of the cosmos." He poetically relates this to the flower, which has within it the sun and the rain and the earth and everything that came before it. Like electrons are made up of all other electrons, we are made up of all other things.

This interconnected, limitless world has offered me many gifts and opportunities to reveal the truth of who I am, who we all are. This journey to the center of my being has asked that I face many so-called enemies and meet my true allies. It has revealed illusions and lies that I have been telling myself in an attempt to cover up the reality.

I have used my chisel of curiosity to chip away at the block of granite, revealing the perfect sculpture that has been there all along. I have faced the messiness of what it means to be whole, remembering that it is out of the messiness that transformation can occur. With my true self taking the wheel, I'm now ready to return home with my treasures, but the journey is not yet over. All this has prepared me to confront my ultimate fear before the utmost treasure can be unburied.

Now that I recognize the inherent connection of all things and know that I'm always okay and no longer need my false protections to keep me safe, I must face the scariest question of all: Can I fearlessly stand in my power and allow you to stand in yours? I'm beginning to realize that the adventure has not just been for me; it's taught me how to fly so I can serve as inspiration for others that they, too, can fly.

PART 3

THE TREASURE

SO THIS, I BELIEVE, IS THE
CENTRAL QUESTION UPON WHICH
ALL CREATIVE LIVING HINGES:
DO YOU HAVE THE COURAGE TO
BRING FORTH THE TREASURES
THAT ARE HIDDEN WITHIN YOU?

—ELIZABETH GILBERT

CHAPTER 8

Facing the Ultimate Fear

Choosing this path with my authentic self leading the way feels foreign and uncharted. It asks that I continue to uncover deep-seated fears and beliefs without the comfort of my previous defenses.

I have ventured through a brave new world and come out the other side in one piece. I have peeled back the layers and revealed that what is within is not as dark and scary as I once thought. I have removed disguises and come face-to-face with my fear of not already being perfect, knowing, connected, limitless. Yet as I prepare to journey back home to my true self—barehanded, naked, and prepared to shine more brightly than before—I notice that some fear remains: the fear that I *am* all these things.

As *A Course in Miracles* says, "The abilities you now possess are only shadows of your real strength." Here I've been running around most of my life scrambling for false ways to feel powerful, larger than life, unbreakable, and eternal. Yet what I'm actually doing is running away from the truth that I *am* all these things, because, deep down, it's pretty damn scary to believe that.

Our human minds like to make sense of things, to create struc-ture and boundaries and expectations. To be who we truly are would mean breaking through all these limitations. It would mean living from a place of complete trust, acceptance, and surrender. We could no longer put ourselves in a nice, neat box (or put anyone else in a nice, neat box). We could no longer use the walls we have built up around ourselves as protection or limit ourselves to a certain identity, belief system, and, ultimately, this physical existence.

This is a terrifying thought. This means I no longer get to make excuses, feel unworthy, dim my light, or pretend to be somebody I'm not. This means I must step into my rightful place as an extension of the divine and reclaim my power. It's a lot to process!

On my way home to my true self, I receive this revelation: "You are still attached to this concept of not enough, which you use as protection against the fact that you are powerful beyond belief. This keeps you from having to honor the truth and live into the greatness that you already are. It keeps you feeling safe."

I now see more clearly how I have clung to this idea of not being enough like a safety blanket, as an excuse for nearly every-thing in my life. Now that I *know* I am already enough, perfectly whole, and complete, what am I still afraid of? I get curious about this inner conflict. What is still keeping me from shining my light and holding me back?

After some exploration, I dig and uncover a belief buried deep inside that having power and love are mutually exclusive. If I stand in my power and shine my light for all to see, I will separate myself from those I love most and be punished, shunned, and all alone. This is a mighty unconscious belief that would keep anyone from fully embracing her power. Remember, I have spent nearly my entire life protecting myself from feeling unloved and disconnected. And, as illogical as it may seem, here's this fear that standing in my power will elicit just that.

Eckhart Tolle offers some insight on this in his book *The Power of Now.* He says we have both personal and collective pain-bodies where much of our fear comes from. "The personal aspect is the accumulated residue of emotional pain suffered in one's own past. The collective one is the pain accumulated in the collective human psyche over thousands of years through disease, torture, war, murder, cruelty, madness, and so on. Everyone's personal pain-body also partakes of this collective pain-body."

As a woman, I carry with me the female pain-body that has been passed forward from the beginning of time. I can see how there's a lot of fear around being in my power if I carry the pain-body of the many women who died for doing so—think of the witch being burned at the stake for speaking her truth, or the Queen being punished by death for having lovers. Fear of standing in my true power goes deeper than me not wanting to upset others or be judged. According to my ego's pain-body, I could *die* for doing so.

This pain-body took root over the course of my life, growing into weeds of fear and shame. I feared "outshining" others even though I found myself excelling at things. On the one hand, I enjoyed the attention I received when I let my light shine brightly. I danced, I performed, I took Advanced Placement classes.

On the other hand, I learned how this separated me from others.

I recall being made fun of and shunned for being "gifted." I was the kid in seventh grade who was taking advanced algebra with a bunch of eighth graders who were already ahead of other kids their age. For this, I was singled out and made fun of. This is how I internalized it: my brilliance was a threat to others and, ultimately, resulted in me feeling hurt and left out. I have carried this shame with me as a deep wound of not wanting to stand out too much. My personal pain-body believed that those who are smart, talented, and good at things get teased for sticking out.

For one reason or another, many of us have covered up our true essence, so even at a young age, when we see others shine, we feel uncomfortable. We judge it and think it's obnoxious. We have accumulated so many disguises to make sure we never stand out or be the bright light we are here to be—so how dare anyone else! I think this is why I was drawn to the theater. It was an acceptable place to shine my light, a safe place to share my brilliance. It allowed me to "show off" and receive praise and accolades, as opposed to persecution and snide comments.

For many years, I thought I chose theater as a way to hide my true self and validate my ego, as if I was afraid and needed to wear a costume to be loved. Now, I see how in many ways I was validating my true self by receiving confirmation of the light within. Of course, I didn't realize this at the time. I simply got a high from the applause, which had me go back for more. I hadn't yet recognized that it wasn't just a performance, an act, a disguise—it was my true essence shining through that had everyone on their feet.

During an Ayahuasca ceremony, most participants are not on

their feet. Walking around while under the influence of the plant can be very difficult. After using the bathroom during my first ceremony, I found myself crawling back to the circle since that was how others made their way back. In that moment, I heard this voice say, "You are capable of walking." But I refused. I didn't want to stand out or seem like I was "showing off." So I continued to crawl. But the plant wouldn't let me get away with that. She said, "There is no such thing as 'showing off' (which is a judgment). It's simply you sharing your gifts with the world."

Grandmother Medicine invited me to stand in my power without fear of what others might think, which, in some ways, is a very egocentric, self-inflated belief—"Look at how powerful I am! What I did caused you to think or feel a certain way!" She had me turn around, go back to where I came from, stand up, and then walk back to the circle.

It was exhilarating. For one of the first times in my life, I felt I no longer had to hide or pretend to be someone else to be okay. And the best part is that no one probably even noticed. This is such an important reminder for me when I get a little too carried away with what others might think. Chances are, they aren't even paying attention; they're busy focusing on their own journey.

This is what it means to become enough—becoming that which you already are, which is far more powerful than you might ever imagine. When you are enough, there is no need to hide or pretend. Yet here is the sneaky part to this whole thing. I was dimming my brilliance, because I feared that if I didn't, I would be seen as a threat and it would cause hurt or pain—I would be all alone and unloved by others. But then I would cast blame on those around me for why I wasn't shining brightly. "Well, if only *he* was ..., or *they* would ... *then* I could step into my light and my power."

I thought if I didn't have to busy myself with their lack of motivation, their fears *then* I could soar! I would even consider ending relationships or distancing myself from my family so that I wouldn't get "sucked in" and could *finally* be the shiny, bright, magnificent being I am!

While visiting Michael's family in Texas one bright, winter day, the bullshit flag was thrown. I was called out on how this is a big, fat excuse and a total lack of self-responsibility. It is no one's responsibility other than my own to be more of my authentic self. It is not anyone else's fault for why I show up the way I do or choose not to. Sure, we hear the importance of who we surround ourselves with and it is still up to me to find that, create that, or shine despite it.

Think about being a lighthouse. A lighthouse doesn't turn off its light and then blame that on the fact that there aren't other lighthouses nearby shining brightly. That doesn't make any sense. The whole reason a lighthouse exists is because it's the only source of light in a given area to guide others. Equally, turning off your light so as not to distract, taunt, or threaten others will only increase the chance that they crash into the rocks or get lost at sea.

> We are all lighthouses shining light on
> the collective sea of unconsciousness,
> and the more lights we turn on, the
> better we all can see.

Shining your light for others to see doesn't imply you are better than them, know more, or are more talented. Shining your light is a confirmation of what each of us is capable of and already possess. It's your duty as a divine being interconnected with all things.

The flower doesn't keep herself from blossoming in all her glory out of fear of what the other flowers might think. The lion doesn't tame his fierceness because he's worried about how other animals in the kingdom will perceive him. The peacock doesn't hide his vibrant plumage just because he's the only one who displays it.

When you live your life shrouded in the veil of not being enough, you think this is why you are hiding—*who am I to shine?* What you ultimately discover is that is exactly what you are hiding—the brilliance of who you are, first from yourself and then from others.

As I journey back to the very thing I have been hiding for most of my life, the anticipation of danger is replaced with absolution. I no longer desire to feel guilty for standing in my power. I no longer want to feel punished or cast out. I practice self-forgiveness for covering up my light, for abandoning my true self for all these years.

This journey to becoming enough is not some out-and-back hike. It's much more akin to climbing a mountain with multiple switchbacks. Sometimes it feels like you're going backward, but when you zoom out and look at the entire picture, you're still making progress and making your way up the mountain. This quote from the *Tao Te Ching* sums it up well: "The enlightened path appears dark, and advancing on this path may seem like retreating. For the path that looks smooth is often rugged." Equally, I'm discovering the enlightened path leads to the revelation that you are not the hiker but, rather, the entire mountain.

Many of us start our journey with the idea that it's an opportunity to be free of all suffering, pain, and judgment—to become "enlightened." We don't like messy. We don't like discomfort so we go out in search of how to avoid it at all costs without first embracing it.

The Buddha teaches that we transcend suffering when we attain *nirvana*. While attaining the cessation of pain is part of the journey, we can't avoid the First Noble Truth—*dukkha*, "incapable of satisfying." We live in a world of impermanence, everything comes and goes. We seek happiness in things that won't last, therefore we remain unsatisfied. So long as you cling to things or seek happiness outside yourself, you will experience *dukkha* and pain.

This journey is not about cleaning up the mess or making things more comfortable. As Eckhart Tolle says so succinctly in *A New Earth*, "You need to say yes to suffering before you can transcend it." The way I interpret the Buddha's teaching is it's not that pain and suffering magically disappear; it is by shifting our perspective and experience of pain and suffering that we transcend *dukkha* and attain *nirvana*. And this miracle can only occur in this moment.

The further I journey up the mountain, switchbacks and all, the clearer it becomes that the purpose of this particular adventure is for something far greater than my own enlightenment. It is to connect more with my inherently courageous self, messy as it may be, so that I can connect more with those around me. It is to trust my inner knowing, as uncertain as it may seem, so that I can extend that trust to others. It is to stand in my power, as scary as it may feel, so that I can empower others to stand in theirs.

Allowing another person—whether she is your spouse, partner, child, parent, or friend—to stand in her own power and make decisions for herself means releasing a need to control.

False power is controlling;
true power is allowing.

Standing in my power means allowing others the same dignity. I can allow them to have their way and still unapologetically stand in mine. There is no manipulation, control, or conversion required. There is tremendous power in witnessing someone for who they truly are, which is not the disguises we so often see at face value.

As *A Course in Miracles* says, "If you perceive truly you are cancelling out misperceptions in yourself and in others simultaneously. Because you see them as they are, you offer them your acceptance of their truth so they can accept it for themselves. This is the healing that the miracle induces." It is one thing to do this with people who are doing things *right* and quite another to extend to those doing it *wrong*. This is where judgment once again complicates things. Just because I don't agree with what you do, say, or how you live your life doesn't give me license to control it.

As I now stand in my power, I trust that others are exactly where they need to be just as I am—not better or worse. I'm letting go of my need to fix them from a newly formed spiritual, greater-than-thou perspective and instead empower them to awaken in their own way, on their own time.

When I first met Michael, there was still a part of me that wanted to control his experience. I figured if I did things the *right* way, I could help him see the light, keep him from experiencing the pain and suffering that accompanies depression and substance abuse.

Three years later, I begin to see it differently. He—just like me or you or anyone else—is not in need of being fixed; he's in need of being perceived truly for who he is. He doesn't need me telling him to stop drinking; he needs me to empower him to courageously stand in his power and to fearlessly accept the consequences of his actions. He doesn't need me to force him into treatment; he needs me to let go of any attachment I have so that he is free to make the choice that is best for him. He doesn't need me controlling his experience; he needs me to trust that the dis-ease he experiences is exactly what it is meant to be, and the path he is on is leading him exactly where it is meant to lead him.

This is what it means to fearlessly stand in my power and empower others to stand in theirs. While I cannot know what is best for Michael's evolution (or anyone else's for that matter), I do know this: He is one of my greatest teachers. Each moment, I get to choose to approach him with fear or love, and either judge him for the disguise he wears or see him for who he truly is.

A Course in Miracles teaches, "When you love someone you have perceived him as he is, and this makes it possible for you to know him." Each day, I practice being true to myself and trust that Michael is capable of being true to himself, in whatever way that happens to look. This certainly isn't always easy, but it's the assignment I signed up for. There is a reason he is on this journey with me.

Another revelation offered me by Ayahuasca is how I have blamed Michael and his relationship with alcohol for much of my "grief." In that revelatory moment while lying beneath the Peruvian-night stars, I was offered an opportunity to feel what it's like to take full responsibility for choosing Michael and co-creating our relationship. It felt so freeing to see how I have created it for my own experience and growth, and how I contribute to it. I also felt so much love and compassion for him in that moment.

Now, co-creation and participation do not equate blame. There is an important distinction here. For much of my life, my desire and ability to offload responsibility at any opportunity has been pretty easy. I'm the baby of the family, after all. I didn't want to make the wrong choice or think it was up to me. But as a co-creator of my reality, taking responsibility is part of the job description. However, taking responsibility isn't the same thing as being to blame. The energy is completely different.

I'm not responsible for your situation or experience of life; *you* are. Equally, you're not responsible for mine; *I* am. It's exhausting when we think we are responsible for others in this way (constantly tip-toeing around trying to control their experience), and we are resentful when we think they are responsible for ours (believing we are where we are because of them). This doesn't imply that we don't affect others or have an impact on them. Of course we do—that's what it means to be interconnected.

Yet being responsible for how we choose to experience or react to something is up to each of us, independently of the other. This is where true power lies. Being in your power means *allowing* yourself to have your experience and others to have theirs; it doesn't mean you *control* it.

As I begin to take full responsibility and let go of my victim mindset (which the ego just loves!), I lighten my load and begin to experience my true power. I acknowledge that I'm responsible for how I feel, react, what I choose to do (or not do), and for all the incredible love, peace, and ease (as well as the pain, suffering, and strife) I co-create in my life.

> Wading into the pool of radical self-responsibility is only uncomfortable for the first few moments.

You might start to clench up and freeze because you're afraid of how cold it's going to be. But when you decide to take the plunge and dive on in, it only takes a few seconds to acclimate, and pretty soon it feels better to be in the water than out of it. By diving in and embracing your power, it doesn't matter what others think, say, or do, because it ultimately doesn't change who you *are*.

While learning to trust in the power of who I *am*, I still observe myself apologizing as opposed to standing in my true essence because of how uncomfortable it feels to do so. It's one thing to know it exists and another to stand in it firmly. During the first few months working on this book, someone asked me how many words I write a day. Rather than owning my process unapologetically, I launched into justification mode.

I did it again while talking with a dear friend when she asked me about my seemingly nontraditional financial and job situation. She lovingly called me out and reminded me that I have no need to defend myself. She wasn't judging me. I was projecting judgment of myself onto her, which then had me doubt my truth and dim my light. This had me question if I have a belief that standing in my power has to look a certain way, like some sort of superhero, as opposed to it looking like being more of who I am at all times—confidently and unapologetically. There is power in observing this pattern of mine, and freedom in no longer feeding into it.

As the spiritual teachings of the *Tao Te Ching* offer, "Those who conquer others have power, but those who conquer themselves are powerful." As I excavate these deep beliefs one by one, I start to notice how, in the past, I equated my power with being able to control others (either by controlling their experience or controlling their impressions).

What I'm starting to experience now is that being powerful doesn't mean having power *over* another; it means overcoming my false self, by transforming one belief at a time. Doing so is what has led me to unearth the many treasures along this journey. Each treasure revealing another, much like my set of Russian nesting dolls. Every time I transform one belief, uncovering a new gem of wisdom, there's another one awaiting me underneath.

I've transformed my belief about what it means to be powerful. It is powerful to feel emotions fully, deal with things head-on, face the truth, accept the consequences, stand up for what I believe in, be wholly present, and be who I am unapologetically. Being vulnerable is where true power lies. Taking radical self-responsibility. Being willing to be with what *is*.

As this leg of my journey nears an end, I complete this stage of my transformation, with my faithful Observer at my side, noticing all of it nonjudgmentally. I am no longer attached to the idea that it's necessary to fix or rid or acquire. I am ready to stand in my power and be in relationship with my innate perfection, deep knowing, and connection with all things.

However, this transformation requires practice and integration—from judgment to pure awareness, from fear to love. While this adventure has taken me from here to there and back again, I see how it's only one stage of my overall metamorphosis.

After spending time in her chrysalis, the butterfly has to emerge and learn to flap her wings and fly. By doing so, I empower you to do the same, to shine your light in whatever way you want to shine it. Knowing that you—just like me—have everything within you. You are already enough.

THE WAVE IS ALREADY WATER. ... IT
IS THE SAME FOR YOU. YOU HAVE
GOD WITHIN YOU, SO YOU DO NOT
HAVE TO LOOK FOR GOD.

—THICH NHAT HANH

CHAPTER 9

Learning to Fly

I have spent nearly my entire life trying to change. I longed to transform myself and, with it, my entire life. I sought out opportunity after opportunity to improve.

I read books, attended workshops, took courses, hired coaches, went to church, read more books, went to more workshops, and listened to podcasts. This seems to be fairly common and a journey many of us excitedly and willingly sign up for. And why wouldn't we?

To learn, grow, expand is why we are here. We are surrounded by others who have tasted the nectar of transformation, and we want to experience the sweetness for ourselves. Yet what I have discovered is that true transformation is more about savoring the flavor, as opposed to getting a sugar rush.

I caught myself in this trap, thinking that the revelations I was collecting along the way were simply a means to an end. I thought the purpose of transformation was to achieve something in the external world—I transform *so that* I can be more successful, have more money, have a different relationship, and so forth. True transformation, however, occurs when our thoughts about these things—money, success, relationships, pain, suffering—change, and we start to perceive them as the "suchness" of life, not something to attain or avoid.

> There is no "end" to achieve unless you
> accept that each moment is the means
> by which to attain the truth and avoid
> the lie, once and for all.

It's transforming the inner landscape that leads to an outer world transformation, but not exactly the way I had imagined. It's not that your outer world necessarily changes in a literal way; it is transformed through your new thought forms. Sometimes this leads to new dwelling places, partners, forms of abundance, jobs, and so forth. But that isn't always the case—or purpose.

While I journeyed through my inner world, nothing in my external world changed at first; I simply perceived it differently. I still lived in the same city, in the same apartment, had the same relationships, went to the same restaurants and grocery stores, took the same walks.

If anything, I downsized—I earned *less* money than before, acquired less stuff. My inner world, however, shifted and I perceived things externally as a reflection of that shift. I experienced contentment with my simple studio apartment. I appreciated the beauty of San Francisco with fresh eyes. I felt more connected with my friends and more accepting of my partner. I was less critical and more cheerful with people on the street. I experienced the abundance of the universe in mysterious ways. I saw the perfection and interconnectedness of all things.

My life situation didn't change; my life *experience* changed. You don't necessarily have to quit your job or move to another country or reach some external definition of success to experience these treasures and "bring them back home."

My treasure chest is full of pure, unembellished gems of wisdom. Now, it's time to begin the process of integrating these shimmering objects into my previous understanding of the world—to find space on my shelves to display these treasures by cleaning out some of my old artifacts. One of the first ones I pick up and evaluate is if judgment isn't in some way necessary for transformation to occur. I mean, without it, how would I evolve or grow? How would you?

For a long time, I was under the impression that I have to be *less than* in order to be motivated to change. I have to think sitting on the couch and watching TV is a sign of laziness; not working out and eating unhealthy food is bad; drinking too much is a stupid decision and a waste of time; and not making more money or meditating enough is due to a lack of motivation. Basically, how I currently spend my time and treat my body is *wrong*. And it is this judgment that motivates the change—right?

Climbing the mountain gave me a more comprehensive view. *Everything* in nature evolves, changes, and transforms. This is unavoidable. Our bodies are transforming each and every second. If you desire to evolve or grow with more intention, then by all means be more selective of what you ingest, how you spend your time, or what thoughts you choose to focus on.

Notice that none of that requires judgment or comparison or doubt or some other illusion of how you are somehow incomplete as a prerequisite. Sure, the flower will evolve or grow differently based on the soil in which it is planted. Equally, the flower is perfectly whole and complete just the way it is and requires no judgment to turn toward the sun.

Yes, change occurs most rapidly when the flower realizes it will wither and die if it stays where it is versus experiencing a little discomfort stretching itself in a new direction. Still, you can observe all this without judgment. You do not need to beat yourself up and tell yourself how worthless or lazy you are.

> The caterpillar needs no judgment
> to become a butterfly—it is simply in
> alignment with the nature of things.

Equally, it doesn't need to go out and obtain more from the external world before it can transform—it has all it needs within and simply reveals it through its metamorphosis. So, too, it is our nature to transform. Being in judgment keeps you from revealing the true nature of who you are, and it's by getting back in touch with this that the natural evolution can occur from a place of love as opposed to fear—which is the only foundation for lasting transformation to take root.

After many years of practicing Bikram yoga, I started to notice for the first time just how badly the voice in my head judged what was happening throughout the class by saying things like, "I'm so weak! I should be stronger than this," or "I'm about to die! I have to leave the room." In the past, I would have resisted the voice for what it had to say and pushed through, or listened to it and then beat myself up for giving in.

On this particular day though, I simply noticed the voice and became more aware of my body and what it needed and, without judgment, did what I felt was best in each moment. That meant sometimes I observed the voice was simply expressing fear or frustration, and I would hold the pose and stay in the room. Other times it meant listening to my body and sitting down to rest without beating myself up. This transformed my practice. I didn't need judgment to make progress.

Much like a caterpillar, your transformation occurs when you start to outgrow your britches—your pants don't magically expand, you need to shed the old pair. You then enter the chrysalis stage where it may appear you are resting when, in reality, your thought forms are rapidly transforming. This is your dark night of the soul when you call everything into question.

Imagine if the pupa could intellectualize like we do—what must it be thinking? Its entire world, its entire *being* will never be the same again. It goes from being limited to crawling around on one small leaf to having wings and being able to fly anywhere! Yet in order for this to happen, it has to lose the form it once knew—the body of the caterpillar. It has got to be thinking, "What the fuck?"

In 2014, I invested a lot of time and money on myself. Along with quitting my job, I hired a coach, travelled through South America, and enrolled in an intensive self-transformation program that lasted many months, which called a whole bunch of stuff into question. In December of that year, I entered my chrysalis; I experienced my dark night of the soul. It was less of a collapse and more like a voluntary removal of the walls.

Still, this deconstruction left me tired and feeling vulnerable. In the process, my ego threw quite a tantrum. She could tell I was on a mission to tear down the walls she had spent a lifetime building out of fear brick by brick. She felt exposed.

"I am sick and tired of wasting so much time and money on trying to improve myself!" she grumbled. "As if anyone out there knows what the fuck they're doing. Yet here I am throwing gobs of money at them to tell me how to live my life. Fuck that. I'm over it. I'm going to live my life how I want to live my life. I'm not some asshole who's going to let people walk all over me anymore. Meet the new fucking me. The one who doesn't give a shit anymore. The one who has been kept secret all these years."

Wow. She was pissed. I don't blame her. As I invited her to share how she felt, these were the exact words that came spewing out onto my journal. I was turning her entire world upside down, bringing everything into question. My old artifacts no longer went with my new decor. The very thing I had spent my entire life doing—looking to others while trying to fix myself—was starting to transform right before my eyes. And it took time for my eyes to adjust to the new perspective.

While in chrysalis, everything changes. The transformation involves integrating the new with the old. Like the butterfly, when you first emerge, you won't fly well—it takes practice and time to learn how to flap your newly formed wings.

It's one thing to learn something
intellectually, and it's quite another
to integrate it into your being.

Let's pretend that the caterpillar might intellectually know that one day it will have wings and be able to fly, but until it undergoes metamorphosis, it is only a concept. You might *know* there is a butterfly within you waiting to emerge, but it is only once the transformation occurs that you will need to start flapping your wings and master the new art of flying.

One summer, while working at a theater camp, I observed this little girl playing on the jungle gym. She would try to make her way across, fall to the ground, and then get back up and try again. Not only was she willing to try again, she was willing to try different ways of getting across the monkey bars until she succeeded and mastered the art of swinging across them.

In that moment, I was reminded just how important it is to play and experiment—especially while learning how to fly. As I find room on my shelf for my new understanding of perfection, knowing that it isn't found outside myself, I gain more confidence in experimentation. Without the weight of the shield I had been carrying around for so long, I am lighter and freer to play and try things out.

This means trying different forms of meditation. Meditating daily for fifteen minutes or meditating for longer periods at less frequent and consistent intervals. I try various journaling techniques, morning rituals, and different types of yoga. I'm willing to recognize that some things may or may not work for me. I no longer get discouraged when it doesn't work the first time around, and sometimes I choose to take a break from something even if it is working. I experiment with my diet—lemon water, caffeine, no caffeine, vegetarian, no red meat, burgers and fries. I experiment with my wardrobe—

landing on anything without a zipper for the time being. Everything becomes an experiment as I explore the newly formed parts of myself to see what works and what doesn't.

Another way I learn to fly is
by *being* more than *doing*.
Sometimes, less is more.

I find that when I avoid the *doing* trap long enough, I start to witness the perfection that already exists within me without having to effort all the time. Part of the false protection I carried around for so long was a shield of constant doing, telling myself, "If I do enough things, then I will reach perfection."

So I started practicing what it feels like to sit in the space of being good with being me. What if I don't have to do anything to be perfect? What if I don't have to clean the house, or send off ten more emails, or complete my to-do list, or even make a to-do list? This doesn't mean I lay in bed all day and never do anything (though there are a few days like this, which is totally fine). It means that I make a more conscious effort to do less.

Making choices in each moment and allowing myself to feel the discomfort of it not being "perfect" becomes my practice. I start with little things like leaving my bed unmade or leaving the dishes undone or resisting the urge to reply to just one more email. I consciously let things be enough as is. The bed is complete with or without the throw pillows placed "just so." My hair is perfect with or without the curls being "just so." My beauty is real whether or not my makeup looks "just so." This doesn't mean I never make my bed or do the dishes or wear mascara again—I simply no longer do it because I think I'm not okay if I don't.

On the flip side, sometimes learning how to flap my wings means putting Nike's famous motto into practice and "Just do it." It's important to practice leaving things undone and be at peace with it as is. It's equally as important to practice showing up in whatever way you can, as you are in this moment. I'm not leaving things undone out of fear that it won't be perfect enough, so why bother—that was the old way. I simply leave things as they are to remind myself that there is inherent completeness, perfection in all things.

Equally, I have to practice doing things even when I don't feel ready. I start a blog before I have a fancy website. I record videos without professional equipment or quality lighting. I write and publish a book without years of experience or an agent. If I had continued to believe that everything had to be "just so" before I would "just do it," I wouldn't have nearly a year's worth of videos and you wouldn't be reading this book right now.

Learning to fly doesn't always feel good, especially at first.

You might notice that your wings are a little sore, or you might experience bumping into things for the first time. That's fine and part of the process. The more often you experience the discomfort and notice how you are still loved and alive despite it, the more you realize that you are inherently enough.

Integrating my newfound wisdom offers me plenty of opportunities to experience discomfort. I have to learn new ways of discerning whether or not to do something and make friends with uncertainty. Dancing with my inner wisdom means trusting that even when I don't know where I'm being led or when I will be spun around, my partner has my back and knows where he's going.

For more than three months, I am led around the United States with Michael with very few plans and a very loose itinerary. We start in San Francisco making our way to South Dakota, then to Indiana and Connecticut where we visit friends, eventually making our way down the East Coast where we park the car in Florida for three weeks as we travel to Peru before getting back in the car and completing the circle.

One day, while heading south, Michael sees that one of his favorite bands just happens to be playing a show in Durham, North Carolina that night. We realize if we take a different route, we can make it in time for the concert. So we do. And it is an incredible show! Our entire trip is based on having a destination in mind and then allowing the perfection of the universe and our inner GPS get us there.

As my faith in these truths strengthen, I eventually become "location independent" and live out of a suitcase, spending a few more months on the road until finding the next temporary landing spot with my parents. With my inner wisdom as my partner, I am twirled around and led backward around the dance floor, trying to keep beat and find my footing with lots of unknowns and a whole lot of change.

I quickly learn the importance of taking just one step at a time. I don't have to know all the dance steps. I just need to know I want to dance and then take the first step. I don't have to have the entire thing planned out ahead of time or get caught up in the "what should/

could/needs to happen." Instead, I am 100% present in whatever it is I'm doing right here, right now. I remind myself that there is no right answer or right choice to make—if my partner adds a spin, I spin; if not, that's okay, too.

Faced with so many different options—like where to stop for the night, when to move on to the next location, what the next location is, where to live, what to create next, how to make money—I remind myself that it's all right to look at the various choices and potential outcomes, but there is no *one* way.

> No matter what I choose or end up
> doing, I'm going to be okay.

Instead of needing to "figure it out" or "know the answer," I'm open and curious to clues from the universe. Sometimes a friend suggests something, or I read about something that piques my interest. I'm open to it and see it as a sign, a form of support, and I pay attention. Whether or not I use it as part of my decision-making process, at least I'm open to it.

Staying in curiosity over analysis helps me with any doubt that arises from the unpredictability of being spun around the dance floor. I learn to simply observe the inner critic any time she creeps in, acknowledge her, and then continue to dance despite her doubt or criticism. I learn to ask, "Am I avoiding or am I allowing?" Am I avoiding the discomfort that comes with learning a new dance (which the ego will do whatever it can to avoid), or am I allowing my true self to move to her own beat and do that which feels in alignment with my essence? When I ask this question, doubt and guilt begin to disappear right along with comparison.

Being in alignment with my inner wisdom means operating from the space of equanimity, which means there is no room to think I should be more or less. I can be different. I can evolve and expand. Each moment can be a new experience, but wholeness and equality does not need, lack, or want for anything. As I integrate my new treasure of Oneness, I wonder how this is true when I experience "horrendous behaviors."

It seems impossible to accept my already immaculate self when I act in unloving ways and just as hard to accept our equality when you do. So I challenge myself to see how acting in such a way does not diminish the truth; it simply means that I have either forgotten it momentarily or not fully embraced it. When this happens, I refuse to see you for who you truly are, or I act in ways that are completely out of alignment with who I am. I might yell at my boyfriend, eat or drink too much, engage in a relationship outside of the one I'm committed to, or not tell the truth.

When I act in ways that feel out of alignment and disconnected from my essence, I feel depressed, worthless, or less than. Equally, when you act in such ways, I feel angry, resentful, or superior. It's not because of the behavior that I feel this way; it's because I have forgotten the reality of who we are.

The way of reintegrating this fact is not by "cleaning up my act" because *then* I will be whole and complete, nor is it expecting that of you because *then* we can be equal. On the contrary, it is by recognizing and accepting our wholeness—our holiness—in this very moment despite the undesirable behavior, which offers me a reminder of how we are all connected and the same at our core.

The way I choose to live my life naturally becomes more aligned with that truth once I accept it. And when I act or behave in a way that is out of alignment—which happens—I can come back to that knowing immediately and refrain from self-loathing or comparing myself with what I might have done or could be, because I'm reminded that everything I can be, I already am. And once I am able to practice this for myself, I can extend it to you as my equal, which means everything you can be, you already are.

Transformation terrifies the ego, because, as Reverend Michael Beckwith says, the ego can't tell the difference between transformation and annihilation. And rightly so. Transformation leads to the death of all thought forms, including that of the false self. The ego, in this case, is like the caterpillar—it sees transformation as its termination.

Thich Nhat Hanh defines *nirvana* as, "the extinction of all concepts, and the extinction of the pain that concepts cause." As you transform your concepts—of not already being perfect, all-knowing, and equal with all things—you extinguish the pain they cause as you realize the treasure that lies on the other side of the fear. I realized this treasure during my second San Pedro journey after asking a simple, yet powerful question my shaman taught me: "What am I avoiding by feeling fear?" The answer? Divine LOVE! That's it. Pure and simple.

When we choose to live in fear, we're
avoiding love.

Now you might think, but why would I avoid love? Isn't that what we all ultimately want? The false self, according to the wisdom of *A Course in Miracles,* mandates that we seek and *not* find. "The ego is certain that love is dangerous, and this is always its central teaching. ... For the ego cannot love, and in its frantic search for love it is seeking what it is afraid to find."

Love feels vulnerable. It requires faith and dismantling the walls you have spent so much time hiding behind. It requires courage to go from being confined to one small leaf to learning how to spread your wings and trust you won't fall when you fly for the first time.

Learning how to fly with my new treasures of innate perfection, inner knowing, and interconnectedness serve as my metamorphosis, which includes multiple deaths to create room for each subsequent stage. Creating space for the transformation to occur means sacrificing my previous understanding.

My resurrection requires I first die unto my fear-based, judgmental concepts and live anew from a place of love—each and every day. It isn't that my ego has to die; I have to die to my understanding of what my false self is and my belief that it is who I am. There is no getting rid of the ego. The best you can do is observe it as often as you can. By bringing awareness to it, you begin to break the hold it has on your life and operate from a more conscious place (as opposed to cruising on autopilot). It's through nonjudgmental awareness that my relationship with the ego is transformed, allowing it to take a back seat so that I can allow my true self to take the wheel and navigate from a place of love.

This has been my soul's purpose all along. With each of the truths this adventure has awakened in me, I am born again into a knowing of who I truly am—an already perfect, insignificant-yet-significant butterfly with the ability to soar.

WHO LOOKS OUTSIDE, DREAMS;
WHO LOOKS INSIDE, AWAKES.

—CARL JUNG

CHAPTER 10

Waking from the Dream

You know that moment when you wake up in the middle of the night while having an incredibly satisfying dream, and, try as you might, you just can't go back into it?

No matter how hard I try to return to the arms of a sensual embrace or an incredible adventure or the presence of an inspiring mentor, I can't. Luckily, the same thing goes for when I wake up with tears streaming down my face and sweating through my sheets in the midst of a terrifying nightmare. So it is with our spiritual awakening. Try as we might, once we wake up, we cannot return to the dream.

Sometimes, at first, all we want to do is go back to sleep. That state of slumber calls to us. There is such comfort awaiting us there. I think of how badly I want to sleep "just five more minutes" every morning my alarm goes off.

Waking up can feel cold, groggy, disorienting, and perhaps a bit apprehensive. Yet when I give into it, finally drag myself out of bed, and have a cup of coffee or do morning meditation, I feel so much better. Things are so much more vibrant from this awakened state, so much more of life can be experienced. Sometimes I need to be silent when I first wake up. I need time to process what is true and what is not true as I come out of my dream-state. Allowing the dream to be forgotten in the early hours of the morning, as we first awaken, is necessary.

> This adventure has been about
> unlearning everything I have learned
> up until this point in my life.

Most people who know me well—without whom I would have no idea how or where I spent many years of my life—probably think this would be pretty easy given how poor my memory is. And while it hasn't necessarily served me during a game of Trivial Pursuit or when recounting a trip I took, perhaps it has served me well as I unlearn those things that are simply illusions.

While my conscious memory often fails me, the truth I received on this adventure will never be forgotten. I may forget the details of when things happened or the name of the person who said something that completely shifted my perspective or the restaurant I was in when I had an epiphany. But it is impossible to forget the essence that has been awakened within me. I may even forget what it was like to *not* know my true self, to sleepwalk through life, but I will never be able to forget what it feels like to be wide awake.

Once you reveal these treasures, they can never be unknown. Once you awaken to a new perspective, you cannot fall back asleep. Once you emerge with your newly formed wings, you can never return to crawling.

That little two-year-old is starting to see herself in the mirror again as the armor is being removed piece by piece. Her true essence may have been covered up, but it was never destroyed. Now, it can shine once again without fear or need of false protection. The journey was about uncovering her essence; becoming that which I already am, always have been, and always will be.

One of the first things I learn returning to the Ordinary World is that being more aware of the already absolute self doesn't mean I won't still experience pain, judgment, uncertainty, or anger. Ridding myself of these things was not the purpose of my adventure. Just like that little girl with a fearless heart sometimes falls down and skins her knees, I still feel pain and sadness.

The difference is that now when I do, I no longer judge it as being *bad* or *wrong*. I feel it, allow the tears to flow, ask for a hug or a bandage, and then get back up with a joy in my heart that can't be shaken, remembering that all of it is exactly as it is meant to be. I see it as part of my journey, my perfection. The quest went from me thinking I am to create a life where there is no pain and suffering to learning to observe the pain and suffering for what it is, knowing that it does not alter the truth of who I am.

Life is not about creating an existence where we don't fall down and skin our knees. It's about taking a spill and not turning that into a story or an excuse for why it's not safe to play outside. Kids are fearless, because they haven't yet had years of conditioning that tells them they ought to be afraid of everything. The journey back to love is remembering that love can hurt. But just because we feel pain or heartache doesn't mean we need to live our lives in fear. We don't get to choose when we experience pain or loss, but we do get to choose how we respond to it—from a place of fear or love.

One of my favorite images for this journey is that of an onion—there are multiple layers to peel away, and some make my eyes water more than others. There are a thousand analogies to use, and they all point to the same wisdom that life is a journey, a process, a remembering.

Reaching this point in my adventure—this layer of the onion—leaves many layers to go. This is why it is so important to have started with transforming my relationship with judgment. Without judgment running the show, peeling back the layers won't burn my eyes quite as badly. Of course, transforming your relationship with judgment doesn't mean the experience won't still sting from time to time.

It's only from a place of non-judgment that you can accept everything as it is and find joy in the eye-watering process of peeling away the layers that no longer serve you. With your Observer wielding the knife, you can face it with more compassion, willingness, curiosity, and love—and less critique, resistance, analysis, or fear.

> Finding joy in the process means finding
> gifts in unexpected places.

One day, I was having a conversation with a dear friend of mine who was feeling stuck about getting a part-time job while building her business. I offered her a reframe, an opportunity to see something through the eyes of love as opposed to fear and, as soon as she heard it, she said, "I have some blocks around that."

But I didn't hear some unconscious belief that was keeping her stuck—like not being worthy. I heard a choiceful forgetting, a resistance to something she now knows to be true and cannot unlearn no matter how hard she tries—she *is* worthy. She tried to go back into the dream-state, resorting to a story that she has to reexamine the belief or clear away the blocks as opposed to remembering she's awake.

It's kind of like you've been living your whole life using a map and only looking at one side of it that has all these difficult mountains and ravines and swamps and cliffs to figure out, resentfully hike through, or avoid.

Then, one day, you realize there's another side to the map, so you flip it over and see a whole new landscape, a whole new way of moving through life. You no longer need to analyze why the one side of the map has such treacherous and challenging terrain. You don't need to first hike all the mountains before deciding to explore the alternate landscape. You need not spend any more time judging the path or trying to figure out how to get across the ravine. You simply need to remember to reference the new side of the map.

Now, that doesn't mean you won't open up the map to the original side from time to time and find yourself thinking, "Wow, this is so much harder than it needs to be. Why isn't it easier? I guess I'm supposed to break through that mountain or figure out a way around that ravine." When you catch yourself attempting to make things more difficult by using the old map, all you need to do is remember to flip it over and allow the river to guide you, moving through the wilderness without judgment or needless suffering.

After my San Pedro epiphany in Peru, it became crystal clear to me just how undeserving I have felt of divine love, because I haven't suffered enough. I recall many times telling myself (and others) that I haven't had enough tragedies or "hit rock bottom" and, because of this, I developed a story that I wasn't yet deserving of salvation.

To top it off, because I hadn't suffered enough (and believed I had to), I decided I needed to create more suffering in my life—hence the need to find a way through the mountain. I certainly couldn't just go with the flow of the river and enjoy life!

The lesson that hit me like a ton of bricks is that suffering is not a requirement to receive the love, peace, and joy that each and every one of us is innately deserving. While it's true that suffering, *dukkha*, is part of life, it's not the destination. My attachment to it and my resistance to receiving the love that is rightfully mine is keeping me from transcending suffering and surrendering to the flow of life.

> The price of admission for divine love isn't suffering; it's radical self-responsibility.

One of the first things you can do is take responsibility for the suffering you have created in your life and then, lovingly, turn the map over. You don't gain brownie points for being miserable—climbing every mountain or traveling to the depths of each ravine. Your suffering doesn't diminish the suffering of others—it simply keeps you from providing the love and light that is necessary in those situations.

The root cause of so much of our angst and dis-ease stems from this belief that we are vulnerable to perceived threats. And I lovingly invite you to question that on an ongoing basis. What if you are okay just the way you are and no longer need to go around avoiding it or proving it in some way?

I remind my ego each time I catch it picking up the shield of judgment in all its deceptive forms—shame, blame, guilt, over-analysis, busy-ness, control—that there's no need. Instead of using my various shields, I practice doing the opposite thing I might have once done in order to prove to my ego that I am already enough and safe just the way I am.

I bite my tongue instead of proving my point or telling you what to do. I say "thank you" and receive the compliment instead of dismissing it or immediately returning the gift. I refrain from saying "I'm sorry" when I feel uncomfortable or am afraid you do. I observe the craving to have another glass of wine as opposed to pouring it. And you guessed it, I'm still okay. The false protection is no longer required.

> So many of us carry around shields to
> feel more significant and whole.

What we haven't yet realized is that in order to reveal our deepest truths, we need to be willing to stop hiding them. I wrote this book as a way of lowering my shield, releasing the old story, and revealing the truth.

As simple as it may sound, all I had to do was bring the story into the light so it no longer had power over me. As Saint Paul says, "But everything exposed by the light becomes visible—and everything that is illuminated becomes a light." I wrote this book to serve as a light for myself and others. By exposing my beliefs, stories, and judgments, I trust they can serve as a light for you.

In the words of Pablo Picasso, "The meaning of life is to find your gift. The purpose of life is to give it away." This gift of mine to serve as a light was validated while reading *A New Earth* by Eckhart Tolle. He says that the contribution of some of the greatest artists of our time is not to offer us a solution but rather offer us a reflection of the human experience and predicament so that we can see it more clearly.

This is my calling as an artist, creator, messenger. This is the call I accepted quietly while sitting on my couch in my San Francisco studio and continue to accept each and every day.

By accepting the invitation, I uncovered my gift—the authentic way I am here to serve others. It no longer needs to be "perfect" or completely different than anyone else's. It also doesn't need to look exactly the same. I don't need to be certain of what comes next. I found that my authentic gift is asking questions and sharing my lessons with others. This way, I give others permission to ask questions and reveal more of who they truly are.

Shining your light by exposing your innate brilliance is kind of like tweezing your eyebrows—the more you do it, the less it hurts. The more often you are willing to try something and learn from it, the closer you get to revealing the profound truths so many before us have revealed and taught, which is only found by reconnecting with your true self—no longer covering it up or apologizing for it.

Just over a year after my ego threw her vulgar tantrum, I experienced a more refined dark night of the soul. While lying in savasana at the end of a yin yoga class in Mexico, I noticed my tendency to start thinking. I observed this and asked the simple, yet powerful question I learned from my shaman: "What am I avoiding by having these thoughts?" Immediately, it struck me that I was avoiding a feeling of detachment and pure weightlessness and, with that, a sense that I am this tiny being in this huge universe. Ultimately, I was avoiding how insignificant I feel. I experienced an existential question many of us have: "Do I matter?" And all this from asking a simple question.

The need to feel important is a driving force in a lot of our human suffering, and the knowledge of not being significant can be quite uncomfortable. Yet the knowing I received in that moment was that while we are specks of dust in an infinite expanse and what we do truly doesn't matter, the paradox is, we *do* matter, we are important. But not necessarily from the ego's sense of self. While lying in corpse pose on that beautiful January day in Rosarito, I actually felt a sense of relief. Finally, I could live and enjoy life.

My shaman's words echo in my mind: "This journey is about engaging in life more willingly and less seriously rather than attaching to the destination." We can have fun revealing these gems, treating it like a playful scavenger hunt. As Martha Beck says in her brilliant allegory, *Diana, Herself*, "Play is the best way for a soul to learn how the physical realm works."

At times, I need this reminder when I start to get a little serious about the journey and overly attached to a certain outcome or indication that I have "arrived." Such as when I find myself looking at every experience as some deep spiritual lesson or looking to how many people I reach as a measure of success or being overly focused on attaining a certain level of wealth—or serenity.

As Thich Nhat Hanh wisely says in *You Are Here,* "The present moment is the destination, the point to arrive at."

It's not about getting to x, y, or z;
it's about being willing to experience
whatever we encounter on the way
more willingly and less seriously.

Life can be one hell of a ride, after all. It's up to you if you close your eyes, grip tight, and hate every minute of it, or throw your arms up in the air and scream in exhilaration.

Journeying to my true self revealed to me the treasure of nonjudgmental awareness. It's hard to enjoy the ride when you're constantly in judgment of it. This serves as its own treasure map to acknowledging and accepting what is, which is where my next adventure will lead me.

With this newfound awareness and allowing the Observer to reclaim her rightful seat behind the wheel, I'm able to experience greater trust and let go of the need to "know it all" or "have it all figured out." I'm more open to love fearlessly, forgive myself and others, and be willing to observe and then let go of the suffering. I no longer need to continuously seek for the next thing that will "give me the answer" or "teach me what I need to know." I'm learning to be good with being me.

As I first received this message of "being good with being you," I started to experience inner conflict. It seemed like I was suggesting you judge your existence as *good*. But that's not the case. The journey to becoming enough and being *good* is one of non-judgment that leads to acceptance—to be at peace with what is.

One day, a dear mentor and friend of mine asked, "How is it possible to be good with being you when the *you* is ever-evolving?" Great question. I started to notice how some days this means non-judgmentally accepting the *me* that feels lazy, grumpy, not enough and, other days, being good with the *me* that feels divine, whole, and fully connected. At first, I had a hard time reconciling this. How can I be *good* with seemingly contrasting, separate *me's*?

After sitting with this question, it dawned on me that both are true. There is an unchanging, constant part within each of us, and that is the "you" that you reveal and discover by peeling back the layers and wiping away the grime that often covers it up. That is what you are *becoming* more of—beginning to *be* that unchanging part you already *are*.

Being good with being you means nonjudgmentally accepting the "you" that is both unchanging *and* ever-evolving. This is the paradox, the illusion of duality, and why you sometimes feel uncertain and full of doubt. And that's fine. It's part of the journey. It's being good with being all that, too.

Much of what was revealed as I hiked up the mountain seemed contradictory: I am insignificant *and* significant; I am perfect *and* human; there is a deep knowing *and* uncertainty in faith; we are all connected *and* separate; we are different *and* the same. True transformation may not require judgment, but it does require a reintegration of these seemingly contrasting ideas.

All these things are true and there is no separateness or conflict—it is only an illusion that there is. Eckhart Tolle points out that this is because language creates duality that doesn't actually exist. We can't speak about perfection without speaking about imperfection.

Judgment also creates duality that doesn't actually exist—right or wrong, black or white, lightness or shadow, good or bad. Things are *seemingly* contradictory because of the illusion we have been living under when, in reality, it all exists simultaneously in all things.

The process of reintegration begins by noticing the seemingly disparate parts for what they are and being willing to look at all of them. The truth is that the parts were *never* separate or disconnected.

We have never been this *or* that, perfect *or* human, connected *or* separate, evolving *or* complete. The ego simply created this illusion over time built out of fear. Without judgment, I can observe all these seemingly contradictory parts of myself.

I now have the courage to go into the basement, dust off the cobweb-covered lid, and pull everything out of the chest. For all my perfection, I am capable of horrific things. For how significant I am, I really don't matter. For all the uncertainty and doubt I experience, I have a deep knowing at all times. Once it is brought into the light, it's not nearly as scary as I had imagined.

Reintegration takes pardon, persistence, and patience. Pardon is to give yourself grace and compassion, recognizing that sometimes it's not going to go the way you thought, or you're not going to get it all done, or you might have a slump day or behave in a way that is out of alignment with how you want to show up. It is so important to grant yourself pardon.

Then there's persistence. Once you notice something didn't go as planned, or you didn't accomplish everything, or you acted in a way that wasn't in total alignment, you pick yourself up and try again and remember that it's all part of the experience. These are the moments where you learn, get to practice self-love, and decide if you are willing to do it again, perhaps experimenting with a different way this time.

Finally, it takes patience. This is a big one for me. Being patient in how long something takes. We don't know the timing or how everything is to unfold—that's part of the mystery. If you were to imagine you do know how long something is going to take, you think you're in control.

Things may take longer than you imagined or not happen in the timing you think they *should*—in business, relationships, spiritual development, and so on.

As this phase of the journey nears its end, I no longer see myself as lacking, not enough, or incomplete. Yet the journey has just begun. Now that I observe what is rather than passing judgment and using false shields to "protect" myself, the question that remains is: Can I accept *all* of it? Am I ready to accept my wholeness, no longer judging any of it as light or dark? Am I ready to embrace my humanity right alongside my divinity? Am I ready to accept the next call to adventure to the Land of Complete Non-Resistance? Am I ready to be at peace with myself and, therefore, at peace with the world?

Once you step out of judgment, you have the opportunity to accept everything as it is so that you can then surrender to the journey. This brings with it a whole other slew of enemies, allies, and treasures—processing shame, learning to live in the both/and, finding your balance. Once you recognize your enough-ness and gain the treasure of being the Observer—trusting your innate perfection, knowing, and connection—a whole new layer of the onion awaits.

This becoming is the beginning, not the end.

Remember that two-year-old with her cute, curled pigtails? Dark hair and dark eyes, shining brightly? Wearing her little blue and red polka-dotted dress? She has returned. Full of trust. Full of awe for the perfection and interconnectedness life has to offer. Full of light and love for everything around her. She once again sees herself as whole and complete. She is love. She is fearless. She is limitless. She is enough.

REFERENCES

Benner, Joseph. S. 1941. *The Impersonal Life.* Camarillo: DeVorss Publications.

Dyer, Wayne W. 2012. *Wishes Fulfilled: Mastering the Art of Manifesting.* New York: Hay House.

Gilbert, Elizabeth. 2015. B*ig Magic: Creative Living Beyond Fear.* New York: Penguin.

Hanh, Thich Nhat. 2009. *You Are Here.* Boston: Shambhala Publications, Inc.

Hendricks, Gay. 2001. *Conscious Living: Finding Joy in the Real World.* New York: HarperCollins.

Laozi. Translated by Brookes, Robert. 2010. *Tao Te Ching: A New Interpretive Translation.* CreateSpace Independent Publishing Platform.

Regueiro, Javier. 2014. *Ayahuasca: Soul Medicine of the Amazon Jungle.* Bloomington: iUniverse.

Schucman, Helen, and Thetford, William. 2007. *A Course in Miracles.* Mill Valley: Foundation for Inner Peace.

Singer, Michael A. 2015. *The Surrender Experiment: My Journey Into Life's Perfection.* New York: Harmony Books.

Singer, Michael A. 2007. *The Untethered Soul: The Journey Beyond Yourself.* Oakland: New Harbinger Publications, Inc.

Tolle, Eckhart. 2005. *A New Earth.* New York: Penguin Group.

Tolle, Eckhart. 1999. *The Power of Now.* Vancouver: Namaste Publishing.

Williamson, Marianne. 2009. *A Return to Love: Reflections on the Principles of A Course in Miracles.* New York: HarperCollins.

ABOUT THE AUTHOR

Amanda Johnson considers herself a bit of a nomad—born and raised in the Midwest, lived in nine cities, and spent time in fourteen countries and thirty-two states (not counting the ones she drove or walked through while hiking the entire Appalachian Trail).

Amanda has spent the past few years as a writer, teacher, and radio show host after more than ten years of experience performing, educating, facilitating, and consulting. Her passion is inspiring others—from second graders to CEOs—and connecting with them. With wit, charm, and eloquence, she gets to the heart of wholeness and making that journey from "never enough" to "always okay."

She shares her message in articles for *The Huffington Post, Elephant Journal, Best Kept Self, MindBodyGreen*; videos; group training programs; and her weekly Being Inspired Radio Show.

You can learn more on her website: www.amandajohnson.tv. She can also be found on social media @beingamandaj.

Made in the USA
San Bernardino, CA
08 December 2017